# Palgrave Studies in Science, Knowledge and Policy

Series Editors
Katherine Smith
School of Social and Political Science
University of Edinburgh
Edinburgh
UK

Richard Freeman
School of Social and Political Science
University of Edinburgh
Edinburgh
UK

Many of the questions which concern us in our social, political and economic lives are questions of knowledge, whether they concern the extent and consequences of climate change, the efficacy of new drugs, the scope of surveillance technologies or the accreditation and performance of individuals and organizations. This is because what we know - how we acquire and apply knowledge of various kinds - shapes the ways in which problems are identified and understood; how laws, rules and norms are constructed and maintained, and which goods and services offered to whom. 'Who gets what, when, how', in Lasswell's phrase, depends very much on who knows what, when, how.

In our personal, professional and public lives, knowledge is a key resource. It matters in policy not only as a guide to decision making but because, in many circumstances, to be knowledgeable is to be powerful. Some kinds of knowledge are created and held by small numbers of specialists, while others are widely distributed and quickly shared. The credibility and authority of different kinds of knowledge varies over time and our means of developing and sharing knowledge are currently undergoing rapid changes as new digital technologies and social media platforms emerge.

This book series is an interdisciplinary forum to explore these issues and more. In short, we are interested in the politics of knowledge. The series encompasses diverse topics, methods and disciplines and we welcome proposals for solo-authored, co-authored and edited books. Please contact the series editors, Kat Smith (Katherine.smith@ed.ac.uk) and Sotiria Grek (Sotiria.Grek@ed.ac.uk) to discuss your initial ideas and outline proposals. Kat Smith and Sortiria Grek are the Co-Directors of SKAPE (the Centre for Science, Knowledge and Policy) at the University of Edinburgh, UK. http://www.skape.ed.ac.uk

More information about this series at
http://www.springer.com/series/14592

Simon Smith

# Discussing the News

## The Uneasy Alliance of Participatory Journalists and the Critical Public

Simon Smith
Institute of Sociological Studies
Charles University
Prague, Czech Republic

Palgrave Studies in Science, Knowledge and Policy
ISBN 978-3-319-52964-6          ISBN 978-3-319-52965-3 (eBook)
DOI 10.1007/978-3-319-52965-3

Library of Congress Control Number: 2017934435

Cover illustration: Détail de la Tour Eiffel © nemesis2207/Fotolia.co.uk

Printed on acid-free paper

This Palgrave Macmillan imprint is published by Springer Nature
The registered company is Springer International Publishing AG
The registered company address is: Gewerbestrasse 11, 6330 Cham, Switzerland

# ACKNOWLEDGEMENTS

The research for this book was supported by the European Commission through a Marie-Curie Intra-European Fellowship based at the Institute for Sociology, Slovak Academy of Sciences (grant no. GA-2011-301060).

I would also like to take this opportunity to thank all my respondents at the newspapers *SME* and *Denník N* for their time, patience and enthusiasm.

Figures 4.3 and 4.4 are reproduced with permission from *SME*.

# CONTENTS

# LIST OF FIGURES

# LIST OF TABLES

CHAPTER 1

# Introduction

**Abstract** A theme of our era is the clash between general and local knowledge; one of its manifestations is the struggle for a new contract between the news media as 'fourth estate' and a critical public to which some assign the role of 'fifth estate', while others doubt the compatibility of the competences displayed by citizen contributors with standards of newsmaking. As journalism embraces a 'convergence culture' that destabilises the social roles and newsroom tasks of journalists, Smith suggests it is precisely by studying marginal, emergent or contested roles that we often learn most about the evolution of professional jurisdictions. The introduction then explains why Slovakia presents an ideal context to study the tensions affecting participatory journalism and outlines the five chapters that follow.

**Keywords** Convergence culture · Fifth estate · Journalism · Marginal tasks · Professional jurisdiction · Slovakia

The optimism that initially reigned about the democratic potential of the participatory web has given way to a more sceptical mood that accuses the Internet and social media of contributing to a rise of incivility, the spread of conspiracy theories or the coordinated manipulation of public debate. Similarly, within journalism, a negative myth of participation (encapsulated in a phrase like 'don't read the comments!') has been gaining

© The Author(s) 2017
S. Smith, *Discussing the News*, Palgrave Studies in Science,
Knowledge and Policy, DOI 10.1007/978-3-319-52965-3_1

ascendancy over the positive myth, which foresaw a new role based on community management, facilitation and conversation with readers. In a situation that is common when a change in the technical division of labour creates a 'role problem' at the level of professions' socially defined mandates (Hughes 1958), we seem to be witnessing resistance to the incorporation of new tasks into journalism and diverging views about whether the competences required to perform them belong to the professional repertoire, together with doubts about whether the competences displayed by 'citizen contributors' are compatible with the standards of newsmaking. Viewed against a larger canvas of the 'pro-amateurisation' of knowledge production, we see essentially the same clash being played out in other participatory settings between specialised and non-specialised procedures, abstract and intuitive ways of knowing, general and local knowledge or expert and lay speech forms. An optimistic interpretation of these trends is that we have cast off some unhelpful illusions about eParticipation (and perhaps about participatory democracy), and learned to treat questions about the democratic, economic or informational value of online discussion as empirical and practical challenges. But this requires contextualised approaches, sensitive to the ways actors enact online discussion, what they make of it and what they value it for.

Drawing on a three-year ethnographic study combining textual analysis, interview methods, observation of the online environment, newsroom observation and survey data, this book describes how two of Slovakia's opinion-leading daily newspapers are questioning the value of online discussion, but (for now, at least) remain committed to participatory journalism and sustaining forms of audience participation that enrich journalism and democracy. Their dilemma reflects an uncertainty among news organisations worldwide about what kind of public or reader engagement they want, for example about the costs and benefits of in-house discussion systems versus social media platforms (WAN-IFRA 2016). Slovakia presents an ideal context to study many of the tensions affecting participatory journalism: tensions about the competences required to participate, over the jurisdiction of professional and amateur knowledge producers, and above all between hope that digital public spheres would be more inclusive and disappointment (within journalism) about public passivity and (within journalism studies) about professional rigidity. Here is a country where the small size of the media market and the linguistic community creates even more pressurised work conditions for journalists in under-resourced organisations; where a chequered history of political pressure on editorial independence fuels constant suspicions about the purity and authenticity of both journalistic and subsequent audience production; where the boundaries around journalism as a profession are especially porous given the better conditions that are often available in marketing and public relations work; where the public has an appetite for online news exceeded only in traditionally news-hungry Scandinavia;[1] and where an unusually vibrant online public sphere has recently become the object of intellectual disillusionment for an alleged downward spiral in quality towards polarised ideological wars which exhibit the worst sides of human nature and social intolerance.

Chapter 2 is devoted to theoretical and methodological issues and introduces three concepts that guide the investigation and underpin the analyses: *routines, argumentation* and *competences.* The daily iteration of routines is the context both for the appropriation and socialisation of technological artefacts and for organisational innovation. Any study of the forms of expression that occur in online spaces needs to come to terms with their argumentative diversity – notably the juxtaposition of vernacular species of argumentation and more specialised ones. Competence, understood here as both aptitude and jurisdiction, is one of the key stakes of online discussion, as journalists, moderators and contributors mutually evaluate one another and in so doing negotiate the standards for and the boundary between professional journalism and public criticism. As key concepts in the sociology of organisations (routines), the sociology of public debates and controversies (argumentation) and the sociology of professions (competences), they offer useful (I would argue essential) entry points into a domain of social practice where action, however emergent and innovative it may be, is nevertheless constrained by organisational, discursive and professional configurations or containers.

Chapter 3 describes the Slovak context and the specific settings for my case studies: the market leader for online news – a European pioneer of participatory journalism – and a newcomer with a business model based on strong reader support as an alternative to dependence on media 'oligarchs'. This sets the scene for the three empirical chapters that follow.

Concerns across the world about the rise of hate speech, incivility, intolerance and vulgarity (WAN-IFRA 2016) have led some newspapers and journals to close discussion altogether (e.g. the *Week, Popular Science,* the *Chicago Sun-Times,* the *Toronto Star* and South Africa's *Daily Maverick*) and others to introduce more restrictive (but also more expensive) forms of moderation and user registration (e.g. the *New York Times,*

*The Guardian* and Slovenia's *Dnevnik*). Against this background it is shocking how little we know about the nature of the work that goes into moderating comments and the experiences of those who do it. Chapter 4 explores the work routines of online discussion administrators as they evaluate comment quality, enacting different 'registers of justification' that appeal to both rule-based and experience-based repertoires of judgement, anchored in a sense of journalistic craft but also diverging from it in important ways.

Chapter 5 describes the conversations between journalists and critical publics occurring beneath newspaper stories, highlighting the frequency of 'metajournalistic' exchanges that enact normative debates about what journalism should do for society and how journalists should do their job. If the tendency to withdraw from participative spaces were to continue, the media would thus forego an opportunity to use comments as an occasion for self-evaluation and self-criticism – an opportunity that is more vital than ever in a context of uncertainty about journalism's future and economic pressure to find a workable and profitable 'contract of communication' with online publics.

Finally, against the background of perceived colonisation of the public sphere by professional political communicators, whose activities accentuate doubts in the public mind about whether sources are who they say they are, and whether what one reads in the papers can be believed, Chapter 6 describes techniques developed by journalists, administrators, bloggers and discussants[2] to defend the 'public sphericules' of online discussion against infiltration, demonstrating how they are both vulnerable and self-regulating.

This book's sub-title is intended to evoke a paradox: that we seem to be witnessing a crisis in the media's ability to represent the public – a cognitive or semantic gulf between the worlds and worldviews of the media as an institution and large sections of the public – which has appeared during the very same era when innovations in information and communication technologies enabled media and public to interact as never before. It seeks to evoke the idea that a 'critical public' might assume the role of a 'fifth estate', both supplementing the role of the media in scrutinising public bodies (Coleman 2001) and turning its critical gaze back on the media themselves – scrutinising the work of the fourth estate (Bernier 2013). It is this double role, in fact, that makes the alliance so uneasy.

Concerns about the porosity of journalism's borders have been amplified by the challenges posed by the digital economy and culture, so that by 2001, Dahlgren, for example, could predict that 'In cyber-space, the definition of "journalist" may soon be merging with a number of other possible information-handling functions' (2001: 80). This process, exacerbated by the precarisation and despecialisation of an increasingly significant part of the journalistic workforce, is one symptom of what has been labelled the 'convergence culture' (Deuze 2008; Neveu 2009). It has destabilised the roles that journalists assume at a social level as well as the tasks they take on at an organisational level, since it 'introduces a constantly changing mix of features, contexts, processes and ideas into the work of individual newsworkers as their employers, organizations and newsrooms get reshuffled under the managerial impetus of integration and expectation of synergy' (Deuze 2008: 112). In fact, scholars have agonised for so long about whether journalism is a veritable profession that Borger et al. (2013) suspect that the professional project of journalism has actually been something carried by external advocates in the academy, of little practical concern to journalists themselves. Yet however heteronomous (Bourdieu 1998), vague (Ruellan 1993) or porous (Carlson and Lewis (eds.) 2015) journalism is, none of these reservations should prevent us from studying it as a profession if we respect Abbott's cardinal maxim that professions are constructed in a system of inter-professional competition and cooperation where the central stake is the delimitation of jurisdictional competences to practice and institutionalise their particular way of knowing and have its products or services recognised as socially valid and valuable. From this conceptual perspective it is the marginal, emergent and/or contested tasks and roles that often tell us most about the evolution of professional and inter-professional jurisdictions: 'understanding the moving borders is essential to understanding changes in the heartland; borders are in fact the central determinants of professional development' (Abbott 1988: 349). Whereas most studies of participatory journalism have focused on the auxiliary roles allocated to or claimed by citizens, audiences and publics in news production, this book investigates two of the new tasks which have been, or are being, appended to the journalistic portfolio as a direct result of the participatory turn that journalism has taken in the digital era. For how journalism reconfigures itself *internally* to accommodate tasks like discussion administration or responding to comments tells us a lot about its changing *external* relationship to its public.

The book offers a novel way of looking at participatory journalism as front-line professional knowledge work, showing how even the most 'routinised' work is replete with situations in which professionals find space for discretion in the very performance of routines. Drawing attention to the strong metajournalistic and metadiscursive dimensions of online discussion in a context where journalism is expected to be opinion-forming, it re-examines the tension between rational argumentation and polemic which is often manifest in a discrepancy between ideals and practice. It examines the enacted competences of both discussants and journalists, each as seen through the eyes of the other, and throws new light on recurring tensions about what count as valid participatory competences when the public is solicited as a contributor to political, policy or expert debates. Amid doubts about the 'added value' of online discussion for both journalism and democracy, it accounts for participatory journalism as an impermanent and always locally constituted arrangement of actors, artefacts, routines, competences and argumentative norms for the production of news and the animation of the public conversations that news generates. In such an arrangement, everyone is not a journalist but everyone can be a contributor.

## NOTES

1. According to a representative survey commissioned for this research (see Chapter 3).
2. I use two terms interchangeably for people who participate in comments to news – discussant and contributor. The former may sound slightly odd in English, given its more common usage in the context of academic seminars, but it is etymologically closest to the usual Slovak word, *diskutér*, the latter is also etymologically grounded in the Slovak context, since the normal term for a comment – *príspevok* – literally means contribution, while it also allows me to make a link to theoretical work on participation in the conclusion.

## REFERENCES

Abbott, A. (1988). *The system of professions. An essay on the division of expert labor*. Chicago & London: University of Chicago Press.

Bernier, M.-F. (2013). La monteé en puissance d'un « cinquième pouvoir »: les citoyens comme acteurs de la corégulation des medias? *Éthique Publique, 15*(1). Available at https://ethiquepublique.revues.org/1077 [accessed 9.7.16].

Borger, M., Van Hoof, A., Costera Meijer, I., & Sanders, J. (2013). Constructing participatory journalism as a scholarly object. *Digital Journalism, 1*(1), 117–134.

Bourdieu, P. (1998). *On television*, trans P. P. Ferguson, New York: New Press.

Carlson, M., & Lewis, S. (Eds.). (2015) *Boundaries of journalism: Professionalism, practices and participation*. Abingdon & New York: Routledge.

Coleman, S. (2001). The transformation of citizenship? In: B. Axford & R. Huggins (Eds.), *New media and politics* (pp. 109–126). London: Sage.

Dahlgren, P. (2001). The transformation of democracy? In: B. Axford & R. Huggins (Eds.), *New media and politics* (pp. 64–88). London: Sage.

Deuze, M. (2008). The professional identity of journalists in the context of convergence culture. *Observatorio, 7*, 103–117.

Hughes, E. (1958). *Men and their work*. Glencoe, IL: The Free Press.

Neveu, É. (2009.) *Sociologie du journalisme [Troisième edition]*. Paris: La Découverte.

Ruellan, D. (1993). *Le Professionnalisme du flou*. Grenoble: Presses universitaires de Grenoble.

WAN-IFRA. (2016). *Online comments: Do they matter?* Frankfurt Am Main: The World Association of Newspapers and News Publishers. Available at: https://www.wan-ifra.org/sites/default/files/field_message_file/WAN-IFRA_Online_Comments_2016.pdf

# CHAPTER 2

# Participatory Journalism as a Way of Knowing

**Abstract** Disappointment increasingly characterises academic and professional interpretations of participatory journalism, but accounts of 'failure' say little about how participation works. Smith treats commenting on news as a socio-technical *dispositif* configured by situated actors through the performance of routines, the enactment of arguments and the recognition of social and discursive competences. This makes it possible to ask, empirically: to what extent do today's commenting sections carry the original participatory ideals? Laying the theoretical groundwork for the empirical chapters of this book, Smith sets out a conceptual framework derived from pragmatic socio-linguistics and actor network theory that enables participatory journalism to be described as a locally constituted, more or less stable arrangement oriented towards the production of news and the animation of the public conversation that news generates.

**Keywords** Argumentation · Competence · Participatory journalism · Pragmatism · Routine

## A Pragmatic Approach to the Study of Participatory Journalism

The object of my research and the subject of this book is not a straightforward thing to define, and in practice it was a moving target. First, the Slovak newspaper system recently went through a period of restructuring

© The Author(s) 2017
S. Smith, *Discussing the News*, Palgrave Studies in Science, Knowledge and Policy, DOI 10.1007/978-3-319-52965-3_2

driven in large part by ownership changes, which caused a staffing upheaval and an identity crisis at my first case study organisation and prompted the foundation of my second. Secondly, the preoccupations of the actors I studied evolved over the course of the three years I followed them (2013–2016). Both case study organisations have a 'project culture' (denoting both a way of organising work and an openness to ideas for projects from employees),[1] and I witnessed a range of participatory projects being proposed and then quickly abandoned, such as for 'hyperlocal blogging' or for an ombudsman post that would have been a first in Slovakia. And thirdly, even at the level of everyday life in the workplace, it quickly transpired that I was studying roles, tasks and activities without established names and definitions, and hence I had to find and develop ways of talking about them that made it possible to have meaningful conversations about them with my respondents in the field. Sometimes that was more effective by adopting indigenous terms (the verb 'admining' is a good example), but it was also helpful to provoke reflection by using unfamiliar, theoretically informed terms in other situations (I had a range of stimulating conversations about the prominence of 'metajournalism' in discussion, for example). The term I eventually settled on to characterise my research object (for example when I introduced myself to interviewees) was participatory journalism.

This is a term which has itself undergone a shift in meaning since it was first coined just over a decade ago. Here are three definitions from some of the most-cited works on participatory journalism:

[Participatory journalism] refers to individuals playing an active role in the process of collecting, reporting, sorting, analyzing and disseminating news and information – a task once reserved almost exclusively to the news media. (Lasica 2003: 71)

The act of a citizen, or group of citizens, playing an active role in the process of collecting, reporting, analyzing and disseminating news and information. The intent of this participation is to provide independent, reliable, accurate, wide-ranging and relevant information that a democracy requires.

Participatory journalism is a bottom-up, emergent phenomenon in which there is little or no editorial oversight or formal journalistic workflow dictating the decisions of a staff. Instead, it is the result of many simultaneous, distributed conversations that either blossom or quickly atrophy in the Web's social network. (Bowman and Willis 2003: 9)

User contributions to the newspaper website. The participation can occur at various stages of the news production process, and it can make use of a variety of tools. Participatory journalism includes comments as well as other more labor-intensive forms of what also is referred to as 'user-generated content' and 'citizen journalism'. (Singer et al. 2011: 206)

In a useful genealogy of English-language academic writing on participatory journalism, Borger et al. note a rising sense of disappointment symbolised in the transition from the undisguised idealism that resonates in Lasica's and Bowman & Willis's early definitions of the term to the sobriety of Singer et al.'s more recent attempt to define participatory journalism in terms of what it looks like and where to expect to find it. They identify three particular 'disappointments' in recent scholarly accounts: 'disappointment with professional journalism's obduracy; disappointment with journalism's economic motives to facilitate participatory journalism; disappointment with news users' passivity' (Borger et al. 2013: 124). They increasingly counteract the hitherto dominant discourse of enthusiasm for the Internet's democratic possibilities and for a renewal of journalism in an era of electronic democracy. The founding works in this body of literature (Lasica 2003; Bowman and Willis 2003; Gillmor 2006; Rosen 2006) indeed had a manifesto-like flavour, heralding a new age in which digital media would either enable the public to produce its own news instead of being dependent on professional journalists and media organisations, or foreseeing a reinvigorated journalism as the facilitator of a more transparent, comprehensive and dialogical reporting that would strengthen democratic participation. Recent studies of participatory journalism have, by contrast, often been attempts to explain why either journalism or the public has not responded as anticipated. Newsroom studies, in particular, have tended to fall into Borger et al.'s category of 'disappointment with journalism's obduracy'.

Borger et al. accuse journalism studies of producing its own 'moral disappointment' by the way it has constructed participatory journalism around a theory of change that was always more an academic programme than it was either a professional or civic project. I argue that even if they are right, they are missing the more fundamental point that it is futile to talk about participatory journalism as a singular phenomenon. It is much more helpful to start from the concrete situations in which journalists meet publics through and within technological artefacts and then investigate whether and to what extent these situated actor-networks carry or resist the participatory ideals that circulate in contemporary socio-technical systems. So while my research object does not map neatly onto any one of the aforementioned definitions, the term nevertheless retains a use-value by connecting a professional practice to a participatory ideal which, in one form or another, encapsulates the hopes invested in the Internet from its beginnings. That allows the pragmatic researcher – simultaneously holding in mind both concepts and their conceivable practical effects (Peirce 1934), both what is said and the situations in which it is said (Chateauraynaud 2003: 73–75) – to adopt an agenda grounded in work and the language of the workplace while remaining attentive to the traces of an ideal or an idea of participation left in routines and discourses. Reciprocally, the latter played a guiding role in basic fieldwork decisions about where to look, who to talk to or what leads to pursue. Sometimes it took me down alleys that parallel actor network theory's maxim to 'follow the actors' but sometimes there was (certainly from my respondents' perspective) a perversity about my choices, in the sense that many of the routines and artefacts I focused on were things that seemed trivial or marginal to their understanding of what news production is about. Such choices were often undoubtedly the unconscious expression of my autonomy in relation to their agenda, but they were also the conscious product of adopting as a sort of counter-balancing maxim Hughes' (1958) advice that we learn a great deal about professions from the way they handle 'dirty work' on the margins of what they define as core competences or social responsibilities. Methodologically, Hughes' maxim entails sometimes looking (or persisting in looking) where the actors might prefer you did not look. This still conforms to the pragmatic exigency to 'privilege the interpretations necessary for the investigation' (Chateauraynaud 2011: 454).

Practically, the research came to revolve around the organisation of online comments facilities, and here the notion of participatory journalism furnished a useful set of questions or frames. For instance, one version of the disappointment account is a judgement that allowing the audience simply to comment on published articles is a weak form of participation or worse, an attempt to confine public participation to a separate space and a post-production phase where it cannot jeopardise the integrity of professional knowledge production (Singer et al. 2011; Paulussen et al. 2007). Yet Graham (2012) has questioned the logic of assuming that public engagement in the early stages of news production is 'somehow more participatory' than following publication. Indeed two of the classical accounts of the relationship between the press and public opinion

(Habermas and Tarde) assume that public debate feeds off an interpretation of events that is already in circulation in the public sphere. This is not to say that other forms of participation further upstream should be discouraged (Chapter 6 describes a case of online public participation in the investigation and framing of a public issue in coordination with professional journalists) but that certain important functions of discussion and conversation in the formation of public opinion have an essential intertextuality to them which requires some primary material as an input. Only then can Tarde's 'infinitesimal variation and recontextualisation' commence – only then does the press 'set off tongues'. Habermas's conception of deliberation is similarly dependent on the prior existence of news as a written or oral text that furnishes 'issues' for public debate and criticism.

In order to understand what kinds of participation online comments facilities on news websites generate it is vital to have good historical accounts of their genesis, configuration and use. Yet such accounts are surprisingly rare. In fact, there is little or no research examining either how one particular model for online reader participation (commenting under the article) became established in most newspapers and other news sites as the global standard, or investigating how local configurations of this standard idea affect the practical translation of participatory ideals (Wright and Street (2007) represent an exception in another domain of eParticipation studies). Before dismissing comments as an example of 'the law of radical potential suppression' (Domingo 2008) or assuming that invitations to comment on news websites are 'only' the continuation of 'Letters to the Editor' sections[2] (Rebillard and Touboul 2010: 329), it is important to ask seriously, as an empirical question: to what extent are comments sections a vehicle for participatory ideals? What kinds of participation do they actually enable? The main claim of this book is to do just that – to test comments' ability to carry some of the ideals of participatory journalism based on a detailed description of how they work (and whose work goes into them) in two cases whose managements have a long history of commitment to one form or another of public participation in the production of news. As elsewhere, this commitment was initially expressed in a diversity of participatory experiments before it converged around the 'comments-below-articles' function. Rather than suppose that this standardisation implies a retreat from radical innovation, I investigate how journalists 'do' participation in their daily work both as comment administrators and as the authors of articles. I consider what roles are available to them when they do so, and I observe how their involvement with comments (whether it is intensive or peripheral) affects their discursive identities as professional knowledge producers. I investigate how the technological artefacts and social relations (always potential sources of resistance) of online comments facilities constrain and/or enable journalists to act in their capacity as knowledge producers. I ask what kinds of participatory journalism get done when journalists interact with the public through a comments facility in settings where it is reasonable to assume a high degree of organisational commitment, but also different forms and degrees of professional 'dispositional' resistance, to a participatory script.

Comments facilities in themselves are neither the incarnation of the participatory myth nor the evidence of its failure to take hold. They are understood here as a more or less open socio-technical *dispositif*[3] configured and reconfigured by specific actors through the performance of organisationally inscribed *routines*, the enactment of *arguments* (subject, that is, to an argumentative constraint) and the recognition of social and discursive *competences*. The empirical chapters of this book offer three different takes on this process of configuration.


## ROUTINES AND ARTEFACTS

My account of participatory journalism will make frequent reference to routines, which are understood here as theorised by Martha Feldman and Brian Pentland (Feldman 2000; Pentland and Feldman 2005). For these authors they are the local, temporary, technologically inscribed solutions to the incompleteness of rules, furnishing an actor with a repertoire of actions for exploring solutions without prescribing or guaranteeing solutions. Their conception of routines is intended to challenge the idea that use and improvisation are separate from design aspects of technological artefacts. These two aspects are, respectively, the live and dead aspects of routines:

> Any organizational routine that involves people, who are capable of learning from experience, is at least partially a 'live' routine. The key distinguishing factor, following Dewey, is that the experience of the participants naturally and inevitably gives rise to learning. In our terms, live routines are generative: enacting them naturally and inevitably gives rise to new actions (performances) and sometimes new patterns of action. (Pentland and Feldman 2008: 240)

Generativity implies a further distinction, recognising that there is a dynamic relationship between two different aspects of live routines that they refer to (following Latour) as ostensive and performative. The ostensive aspect of routines consists of the abstract patterns or ideal-typical understandings that routine performers use as a guide or script, whereas the performative aspect refers to the time- and place-specific instantiations of the 'same' routine – the routine as practised. The crucial point (and here their conceptual apparatus borrows from structuration theory as much as actor network theory) is that the performers are in no way excluded from the definition of ostensive routines (Pentland and Feldman 2005: 795). This recursivity is the mechanism through which the generative property of routines is assured.

Abbott, whose approach to the sociology of professions is another of this book's key theoretical references, understands routines more conventionally. Mostly, he refers to them in the context of 'routinisation' (e.g. Abbott 1988: 51), understood in the sense of turning a repeated pattern of action into repetitious, unchanging and unreflected sequences of actions. For Abbott, therefore, routinisation is the antithesis of professionalism (professional inference, to be precise) and is thus conceived of as a prelude to a task's excommunication from the professional repertoire, either through delegation to a subsidiary semi-professional group or through its capture by a rival occupational group that is able to convince the relevant audiences that it can perform the task more efficiently or more cheaply than the profession that originally claimed jurisdiction. While these are important processes in the development of professions (and have some relevance for understanding the jurisdictional claims of journalism towards online discussion), they should not blind us to a range of situations in which professionals mobilise routines and rely on them to accomplish work which is not in the process of being outsourced or deprofessionalised, but stands a chance, at least, of being integrated within their core activities.

In actual fact, what Abbott implies by routinisation is what Pentland & Feldman would call turning something into a 'dead' routine, which implies the domination of action by artefacts. Pentland & Feldman agree that we need 'to consider the role of artifacts in routines quite carefully, because artifacts are at the center of design processes' (Pentland and Feldman 2008: 242). Artefacts influence either the ostensive or the performative aspects of (live) routines but at the same time they stand apart from routines and can be adopted, rejected or adapted – differently 'enrolled' – by participating actors, just as they can impose stronger or weaker constraints on action depending on their affordances. Actors let themselves be guided by these objects to a greater or lesser extent when performing routines (Boltanski 1996). Sometimes they resist the inscribed standards. Empirically it is therefore instructive to look for discordances between the ostensive and performative aspects of routines on the one hand and artefacts on the other: in doing so we learn a lot about organisations' strengths and weaknesses (Pentland and Feldman 2005: 809). I argue, in addition, that actors' attitudes towards artefacts reveal the existence and exercise of professional discretion: while the extreme case of routinisation that is automation limits or eliminates discretion, professional work is replete with situations in which professionals find space for discretion in the very performance of routines.

## ARGUMENTATION

Journalism presently finds itself struggling to come to terms with the limitations of its 'informational' paradigm that prevailed in the twentieth century. The dominant discursive register of this paradigm was objective, factual reporting (selection and framing) of events, sometimes accompanied by the logical argumentation of the journalist as 'critical expert' (Charron 1995). Value-based, ideological and polemical forms of argumentation were confined to special rubrics (editorials and opinion). One of the characteristic features of participatory journalism seems to be an accommodation of a far broader repertoire of argumentation styles (not just from 'citizen' contributors). One of its other characteristics is a reflexive, metadiscursive attention to argumentation that one finds in the discussion itself, in the discussion rules and in writing about participatory journalism. This can be viewed as an attempt to come to terms with the problem of accommodating new forms of audience participation within existing journalistic paradigms.

Take, for example, the discussion rules. Most consist essentially of lists of banned speech forms (e.g. obscenities, personal threats and defamation, libellous or fraudulent remarks, racist and sexist speech, advertising and spam). My first case study bucks this trend by also providing positive definitions for participants: its general discussion rules appeal for 'intelligent debate' and its special rules for pre-moderated discussion begin by stating that in these types of discussions 'only contributions that bring new relevant information or well-argued opinions will be passed'. Although relatively few discussions are pre-moderated (largely for capacity reasons), we can take this as an indication of the newspaper's strongest argumentative ideals with respect to reader participation. It is notable how it places comments in a position that straddles the classical journalistic division between facts and opinion, news reports and editorials, or critical expertise and value-based argumentation: participants may choose either discursive identity. It is also notably ambiguous: what counts as a 'well-argued opinion'? It is likely that Toulmin's pragmatic definition of argument as any combination of a proposition followed by a justification (Toulmin 1958) is insufficient.[4] These types of questions are latent whenever notions of arguments or argumentation are normatively invoked, as they often are by discussants and journalists in the comments and in relation to the comments.

The pre-moderated discussion rules were actually derived from a special codex written by the head of the science desk, who explained in a January 2014 blog post[5] why comments to science news were going to be pre-moderated:[6] 'the discussion has often resembled a pub debate, where people argued by feelings instead of facts'. It was this tendency that he sought to counter with the advent of moderation. Yet the ostensive commitment to a scientific model of argumentation (including, for example, a recommendation to 'cite scientific studies in specialist scientific magazines when formulating your argument') is nuanced further on where one reads that acceptable argumentation can also include 'relevant direct personal experience' and 'polemic', as long as the latter is 'impersonal'. In a survey of active discussants at both case study sites,[7] I tried to find out what forms of argumentation they appreciated and recognised. I asked people to characterise real and ideal discussion, including some of the key-words from the moderated discussion rules as response options. Responding about their own discussion tastes, 'logical argumentation' was the single most popular option, chosen by over 80% of respondents (followed by 'expert opinion' with around 75% and 'new information' with around 55%). When I asked them to characterise the real discussions on the two websites, the two most popular categories were 'conflicts of opinion' (65%) and 'emotional reactions' (just under 50%), while less than 15% included 'logical argumentation' among the four types they could choose. By contrast, just 2% of respondents included 'emotional reactions' and 10% 'conflicts of opinion' in their image of the 'ideal' discussion. This evidence is difficult to interpret. On the one hand, the most active discussants on the two websites endorse the view that people should not 'argue by feelings instead of facts', and most of them would even rule out polemical debate ('conflicts of opinion'), which the moderated discussion rules accept as legitimate (when it steers clear of personal attacks). On the other hand, however, they selected these two categories as the most characteristic traits of the real discussion, in which, let us not forget, they participate regularly and intensively.[8] That they testify to a shortage of logical argumentation should come as no surprise: countless 'e-deliberation' studies, influenced by Habermasian ideals of the public sphere and Rawlsian political philosophy, have lamented the absence of rational or logical argumentation in news comment areas (and other online discussion spaces). That they continue to uphold this as the number one ideal is at first sight surprising in view of their long-term participation in a space where they say it is absent. But the tension between valuing lay speech forms for their profaneness and expecting some minimal capacity for public expression lies at the heart of most online and offline *dispositifs* for public participation (Wojcik 2008), so we should not be surprised to find it even in the metadiscourse of discussion participants (taking their survey responses as a form of metadiscourse).

It is precisely these 'metadiscursive tensions' that I seek to explore and perhaps explain in making argumentation a key conceptual theme of the book, and to do so I employ several heuristic strategies. First, I draw parallels between contemporary participatory journalism and an earlier historical paradigm of journalism, in which argumentation styles were more varied and intermingled – the journalism of opinion that characterised nineteenth century North American newspapers (Brin et al. 2004) and which I argue is still quite strongly anchored as a model of 'serious' journalism in the Slovak context. Some features of participatory journalism, I suggest, can be seen less as a new genre than as a restoration of latent styles of journalism that have their origins in the nineteenth century opinion press, but which were marginalised by the dominant ideology of objectivity and neutrality in most twentieth century newspapers. Secondly, I argue for a pragmatic rather than normative approach, drawing on currents in the theory of argumentation that are interested in its 'everyday' forms but which are agnostic about which types of arguments are 'best', and thus rehabilitate as worthy objects of study conflictual forms like polemic or narrative forms like witnessing. This tradition – influenced by a francophone current in linguistics and discourse analysis that views argumentation not a specific class of discourse, but instead views every speech act as intrinsically argumentative when it is 'linguistically marked' and implicates the speaker (Ducrot 1984; Amossy 2006 [2000]) – recognises and accepts gradations of argumentation extending outwards towards 'existential' tests that a priori exclude agreement (Boltanski 2009), types that are excluded from both the normative conceptions of (modern) journalists and the Habermasian ideal of the public sphere. Methodologically it relies on the many ways in which participants in public affairs maintain a metadiscursive dialogue that accompanies their disputes and serves to qualify the force of their arguments intersubjectively (Chateauraynaud 2003). They often tell us (in telling each other) what counts as a good argument.

Finally, I also want to keep in mind questions of institutions and institutionalisation. Although non-rational forms of argumentation are usually delegitimised if not excluded from institutionalised public arenas (Wojcik 2008), there are important exceptions. Doury (1999) shows on the example of court transcripts that institutions can value argumentative competences that do not conform to standards of deliberative rationality: in court, arguments are often expected to be ad hominem (lawyers themselves use them to either accord or refuse credibility to a witness), and the innocence of an 'incompetent' argumenter (like a child) sometimes adds credibility to their pronouncements because argumentative rhetorical skills are treated by this *dispositif* as a means not an end (and thus open to abuse). Similarly, there are certain arenas and *dispositifs* that admit more conflictual forms of expression, parliamentary chambers and newspaper and television debates being notable examples (Chateauraynaud 2011). Online discussion itself has been construed as the apotheosis of trends towards polemical discourse already well-inscribed in the classical modern mass-media system, where citizens merely take up the baton from journalists in expressing and amplifying dissensus rather than seeking consensus (Amossy 2011a, b). All these precedents might be useful for understanding how online discussion to news can in fact work as a technical *dispositif* for valorising vernacular and less 'polite' forms of argumentation that are not automatically accorded validity by deliberative institutions.

## COMPETENCES

Opening the gates at online newspapers to essentially unfiltered user contributions like post-moderated comments on the news raised the question about the skills and competences necessary to produce content that is worthy of publication on a highly visible news site (even if it is relegated to a space 'below the line'), to engage in meaningful discussion about the news and ultimately to participate in an important part of the political process – the construction of a continually running account of social reality and the framing of public issues or problems. This relates to broader debates in political philosophy about the political, civic, discursive and communicational competences needed for effective participation in a democracy. The Internet aroused both hopes that 'digital democracy' might be more inclusive than traditional democracy and fears that such a newly activised population would lack the necessary political competences so that online arenas like discussion forums would be just 'a political playground for those incapable of participating in traditional political arenas' (Christensen and Bengtsson 2011: 897): the Internet might thus depoliticise participation. Christensen & Bengtsson found that this was not the case in Finland, where online activists (defined partly by participation in online political discussion) 'tend[ed] to be as capable as or even more so than active citizens who only engage in more traditional offline activities' in 2007 (ibid.: 912).

The problem with these types of studies, however, is the strong normative assumptions that lie behind the definitions of competence used. In political science competence is usually measured by proxies such as factual knowledge about political systems, subjective feelings of political efficacy (a sense of influence), education and media use/literacy, all of which reflect conventional, elitist understandings of what it takes to act effectively as a political citizen. For some observers, however, digital democracy shifts the goalposts in the sense that its full development requires citizens and their interlocutors in political and media circles to learn a range of new skills as well as to unlearn some of the competences that had come to dominate the twentieth century public sphere: 'Citizens of the digital age will need to learn new skills. Good public deliberation amounts to more than an equation between technology and civic space. People need to learn how to argue. After a century which culminated in the anti-eloquence of the US "shock-jock" and the banal presidential debates of recent years, it is time for skills of speaking, chairing, listening, summarizing and reflecting to be acquired'. (Coleman 2001: 124). Coleman, nonetheless, is still defending a deliberative ideal and apparently (with the negative reference to shock-jocks) rejecting certain polemical forms of argumentation. There are others who argue that if we are to realise the potential of a quantitative expansion of the democratically active population through online channels we need to widen the argumentative net or relax conventional 'quality thresholds'. Thus Heikkilä and Kunelius (1998: 80) suggest 'it may be that criteria set for what is reasonable and constructive discussion suit the educated and relatively well paid journalists and their peers, but probably not all citizens', so that even if 'public participation requires certain cultural and social competences', new tools and arrangements should take account of the fact that these 'are not evenly distributed in societies'. Reflecting currents in political science that reject the idea that rational argumentation is the sole legitimate mode of political and civic participation, these critics challenge the idealisation of the 'informed citizen', which, according to Schudson, has served only to weaken efforts to create a more participatory, democratic civic life by creating impossible intellectual demands on citizens and stripping politics of its emotional mobilising forces (Schudson 1998). A plurality of discursive registers like witnessing, narrativisation, polemic, conflictualisation and implication (Duchesne et al. 2003b) are thus counterposed to rational argumentative competences by scholars as well as political activists who advocate alternative conceptions of the public sphere to Habermas's. I do not take a position in these normative debates except to concur with Wojcik (2008: 4) that in nearly every participatory *dispositif* (online or not) lies 'an inherent tension between the fact that an individual was solicited in their capacity as a layperson and the expectation that they will nonetheless be capable of public expression and opinion formulation'.[9] My contribution to the study of civic, participatory competences is not to attempt to measure them but to study the metadiscourse on competences that accompanies different aspects of the practice of online discussion: to study how competences are being recognised and mutually evaluated in online discussion.

Throughout the book I turn the lens in both directions, examining the enacted competences of both discussants and journalists, each as seen through the eyes of the other. Chapter 4 thus investigates what discussion administrators expect of participants by way of criteria for acceptable speech, while Chapter 5, through a study of metajournalistic exchanges taken from comments threads, investigates how online discussion is used by a critical public to judge the competence of journalists (both as journalists and as discussion participants) as well as to contest the jurisdictional competence of the media, that is, the historical enclosure of part of the public sphere by professional knowledge producers. For the second meaning of the term competence refers to a profession's right to practice in, or – in the case of knowledge professionals – provide an authoritative account of, a certain region of the social space. This is undoubtedly the most disconcerting element of participatory journalism for the profession to come to terms with: the adjustment it implies to the competence-as-jurisdiction of journalists to chronicle and interpret reality and to the existing contract of communication with readers, as they claim expanded participatory rights in news production. Sometimes, as described in Chapter 6, an effective accommodation based on competence-sharing can be realised, if only in 'emergency' situations, when a collective performance is necessary to protect the authenticity of online participatory spaces.

## NOTES

1. The second case study organisation was actually called *Project N* during its pre-launch phase.
2. Such an assumption would be equally reductionist on both sides of the equation.
3. I use Foucault's term (1977: 299), which is sometimes translated as 'arrangement' or 'apparatus', neither of which quite captures the heterogeneity that he insists on in his definition.
4. In Chapter 4 we will see how discussion administrators are far from neutral about the registers of justification that, when allied to a proposition, confer argumentative status, distinguishing, for instance, between justifications that are purely value-based and those grounded in factual evidence or logical reasoning.
5. http://tech.sme.sk/c/7057850/preco-budu-diskusie-pod-textami-o-vede-na-sme-moderovane.html [accessed 8.7.16].
6. Comprehensive pre-moderation, even within a single rubric, was a short-lived experiment.
7. The most active 200 discussants on each portal were solicited by email in the same random week in late 2015. Fifty-seven questionnaires were returned at Case Study 1 and seventy-five at Case Study 2. The results are available (in Slovak) here: https://drive.google.com/file/d/0B3_fNKXr3DkMLUNhRzhMLTFaMkU/view (for Case Study 1) and here: https://a-static.projektn.sk/2015/12/Dotaznik_N_vysledky.pdf (for Case Study 2).
8. Many of the active discussants at Case Study 1 have accounts that are more than 10 years old, and have written several thousand discussion contributions.
9. For a more extended discussion of how civic competence has been reconceptualised in response to the challenges of e-democracy I refer the reader to her review.

REFERENCES

Abbott, A. (1988). *The system of professions. An essay on the division of expert labor.* Chicago & London: University of Chicago Press.

Amossy, R. (2006 [2000]). *L'argumentation dans le discours.* Paris: Armand Colin.

Amossy, R. (2011a). Polemical discourse on the Net: 'Flames' in argumentation. *ISSA Proceedings 2010,* Rozenberg Quarterly. Available at: http://rozenberg quarterly.com/issa-proceedings-2010-polemical-discourse-on-the-net-flames-in-argumentation/ [accessed 9.7.16].

Amossy, R. (2011b). La coexistence dans le dissensus. *Semen,* 31. Available at: http://semen.revues.org/9051 [accessed 16.2.16].

Boltanski, L. (1996). Point de vue de Luc Boltanski. In: L. Boltanski, F. Chateauraynaud & J.-L. Derouet, Risques Collectives et Situations de Crise (CNRS) *Alertes, affaires et catastrophes. Logique de l'accusation et pragmatiques de la vigilance? Actes de la cinquième séance du Séminaire du programme.* Grenoble: Maison des sciences de l'homme: 14–51.

Boltanski, L. (2009). *De la critique: précis de sociologie de l'émancipation.* Paris: Gallimard.

Borger, M., Van Hoof, A., Costera Meijer, I., & Sanders, J. (2013). Constructing participatory journalism as a scholarly object. *Digital Journalism, 1*(1), 117–134.

Bowman, S., & Willis, C. (2003). *We media: How audiences are shaping the future of news information.* The Media Center at the American Press Institute. Available at: http://www.hypergene.net/wemedia/weblog.php [accessed 9.7.16].

Brin, C., Charron, J., & De Bonville, J. (Eds.) (2004). *Nature et transformation du journalisme. Théorie et recherches empiriques.* Laval (Québec): Les presses de l'université Laval.

Charron, J. (1995). La reconnaissance sociale du pouvoir symbolique des journalistes politiques. *Hermès, 16,* 229–240.

Chateauraynaud, F. (2003). *Prospéro. Une technologie littéraire pour les sciences humaines.* Paris: CNRS ÉDITIONS.

Chateauraynaud, F. (2011). *Argumenter dans un champ de forces. Essai de balistique sociologique.* Paris: Éditions PÉTRA.

Christensen, H., & Bengtsson, A. (2011). The political competence of Internet participants. *Information, Communication & Society, 14*(6), 896–916.

Coleman, S. (2001). The transformation of citizenship?' In B. Axford & R. Huggins (Eds.), *New media and politics* (pp. 109–126). London: Sage.

Domingo, D. (2008). Interactivity in the daily routines of online newsrooms: Dealing with an uncomfortable myth. *Journal of Computer-Mediated Communication, 13*(3), 680–704.

Doury, M. (1999). Les procédés de crédibilisation des témoignages comme indices des normes argumentatives des locuteurs. In E. Rigotti (Ed.), *Rhetoric and argumentation, Proceedings of the International Conference, Lugano*, Tübingen: Niemeyer: 167–180.

Duchesne, S., Haegel, F., Braconnier, C., Hamidi, C., Lefébure, P., Maurer, S., & Scherrer, V. (2003b). Politisation et conflictualisation: De la competence à l'implication. In P. Perrineau (Ed.), *Le désenchantement démocratique* (pp. 107–129). France: Editions de l'Aube.

Ducrot, O. (1984). *Le dire et le dit*. Paris: Éditions de Minuit.

Feldman, M. (2000). Organizational routines as a source of continuous change. *Organization Science*, *11*(6), 611–629.

Foucault, M. (1977). *Dits et écrits, tome 2*. Paris: Gallimard.

Gillmor, D. (2006). *We the media: Grassroots journalism by the people, for the people*. Sebastopol, CA: O'Reilly.

Graham, T. (2012). 'Talking back but is anyone listening? Journalism and comment fields. In C. Peters & M. Broersma (Eds.), *Rethinking journalism: Trust and participation in a transformed media landscape* (pp. 114–127). London: Routledge.

Heikkilä, H., & Kunelius, R. (1998). Access, dialogue, deliberation. Experimenting with three concepts of journalism criticism. *Nordicom Review 1*, 71–84.

Hughes, E. (1958). *Men and their work*. Glencoe, IL: The Free Press.

Lasica, J. (2003, Fall 2003). Blogs and journalism need each other. *Nieman Reports*, 70–74.

Paulussen, S., Heinonen, A., Domingo, D., & Quandt, T. (2007). Doing it together: citizen participation in the professional newsmaking process. *Obervatorio*, *1*(3), 131–154.

Peirce, C. (1934). *Collected papers of Charles Sanders Peirce, Volume V: Pragmatism and pragmaticism*. Cambridge, MA: Harvard University Press.

Pentland, B., & Feldman, M. (2005) Organizational routines as a unit of analysis. *Industrial and Corporate Change*, *14*(5), 793–815.

Pentland, B., & Feldman, M. (2008). Designing routines: On the folly of designing artifacts, while hoping for patterns of action. *Information and Organization*, *18*, 235–250.

Rebillard, F., & Touboul, A. (2010). Promises unfulfilled? 'Journalism 2.0', user participation and editorial policy on newspaper websites. *Media, Culture & Society*, *32*(2), 323–334.

Rosen, J. (2006) *The people formerly known as the audience*. *PressThink*. Available at: http://archive.pressthink.org/2006/06/27/ppl_frmr.html [accessed 9.7.16].

Schudson, M. (1998). *The good citizen: A History of American civic life*. New York: The Free Press.

Singer, J., Hermida, A., Domingo, D., Heinonen, A., Paulussen, S., Quandt, T., Reich, Z., & Vujnovic, M. (2011). *Participatory journalism. Guarding open gates at online newspapers.* Malden, MA and Oxford: Wiley-Blackwell.

Toulmin, S. (1958). *The uses of argument.* Cambridge: Cambridge University Press.

Wojcik, S. (2008). Compétence et citoyenneté. Esquisse d'une analyse critique des travaux sur les dispoditifs participatifs en face-à-face et en ligne. In: *La parole profane: nouveaux acteurs et nouveaux dispositifs discursifs,* Colloque de la Société Québécoise de Science Politique. Montréal: Available at. https://halshs.archives-ouvertes.fr/hal-00485916/ [accessed 9.7.16].

Wright, S., & Street, J. (2007). Democracy, deliberation and design: The case of online discussion forums. *New Media & Society, 9*(5), 849–869.

# CHAPTER 3

# Contextualising the Research Setting

**Abstract** Several factors make Slovakia an interesting place to study participatory journalism: the resurgence of political and economic threats to editorial independence, intense competitive pressures and an unusually strong public appetite to read and discuss the news online. A representative poll commissioned for this book suggests that for commenting on news websites, Slovaks are European leaders. Participation needs to be understood in the context of a media system where the journalism of opinion is the paradigm for the serious press. Smith sets the scene for the later empirical chapters of this book, introducing two Slovak newspapers committed, in different ways, to participation. They are the settings in which this book studies how the current industry standard for participation – comments below articles – works and how it might be reconfigured.

**Keywords** Comments · Online discussion · Journalism of opinion · Journalistic paradigm · News website · Slovakia

Boczkowski's study of online news production 'in the south' (2010) showed that tendencies in parts of the global periphery (from a North American or west European point of view) can illuminate some critical trends affecting the media (the big theme of his book is imitation). Could we not make a similar case for studying many aspects of newswork and newsmaking 'in the east', where the press has had to cope with a lethal

© The Author(s) 2017
S. Smith, *Discussing the News*, Palgrave Studies in Science,
Knowledge and Policy, DOI 10.1007/978-3-319-52965-3_3

combination of oligarchisation and hypercompetition and where the pressures on journalists and media organisations to reconfigure their work are especially intense? The setting for this book, Slovakia, is, I contend, a particularly interesting place to study *participatory* journalism, since there is an unusually intense public appetite for discussing the news and yet, as in the rest of the world, the comparatively low willingness to pay for access to news online threatens the very viability of many newspapers.

Chapters 4–6 give three ethnographic accounts of participatory journalism as practised in two of Slovakia's opinion-forming daily newspapers, selected for study because of their commitment to facilitating public debate. *SME* is the country's second or third largest daily as measured by average daily print readership figures (reaching around 7% of the population in early 2016) but the leading online news portal (with just over 2 million real users in May 2016).[1] *Denník N* is a smaller newspaper, the 8th largest by average daily print audience (reaching around 2% of the population) and about its 10th largest news portal (with nearly 600,000 real users in May 2016). It is an interesting counterpoint to *SME* both because of the size difference (which impacts on the human and technical resources available for participatory journalism) and as a new venture formed with an explicit commitment to editorial independence (which impacts on the type of 'contract' with readers that is conceivable or desirable). This chapter provides some background about the Slovak media system, about the history of the two newspapers and their arrangements for doing participatory journalism and, firstly, about Slovaks' relationship to the news.

In order to get some internationally comparable data on Slovaks' media consumption and participation habits I commissioned a public opinion survey (carried out by the FOCUS agency as part of its December 2015 omnibus survey) making use of several of the questions from the Reuters Institute's annual Digital News Report (DNR),[2] since Slovakia is not yet included in their survey.[3] The results confirm that Slovaks are heavy news website users. Figure 3.1 compares the percentage of respondents in different countries who said that during the past week they had come across a news story by directly accessing a news website.[4] Only three Scandinavian countries – where newspapers traditionally play a very important role in public life, and have much higher sales figures – rank ahead of Slovakia on this measure of online news consumption. The DNR and my survey also asked about accessing online news stories via other channels: search engines, social media, email, mobile alerts and news aggregators. There is no widely used news aggregator in the Slovak market, but on all the other indicators Slovakia would come in between 8th and 10th

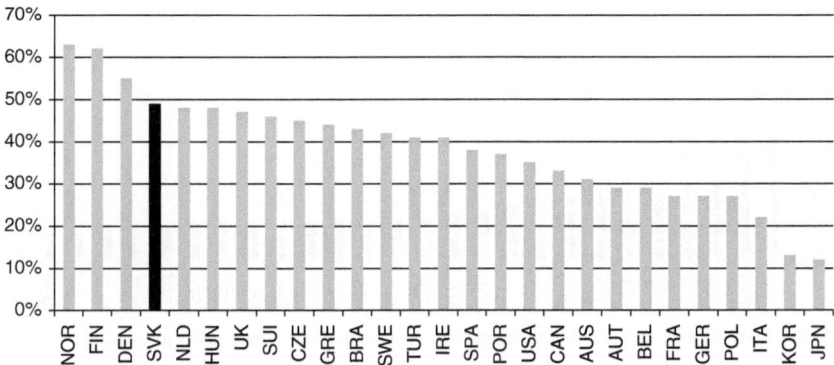

**Fig. 3.1** Accessing news online via news websites *Sources*. Slovakia: representative poll of 1,004 adults, 1–8 December 2015, by FOCUS for Institute for Sociology SAV. International: Reuters Institute Digital News Report 2016.

compared to the 26 countries included in the 2016 DNR. Slovaks are thus above-average consumers of online news by all available channels, but their brand awareness – a strong habit of going directly to news sites – is what marks them out, according to my survey results.

Slovaks are also very active participants in news coverage. In Fig. 3.2 I compare the percentages of participatory news users in Slovakia and in the countries surveyed for the 2016 DNR. Participation is defined as sharing, rating, liking, commenting or talking about a news story (on- or offline) or blogging about a news issue. Around 72% of Slovak

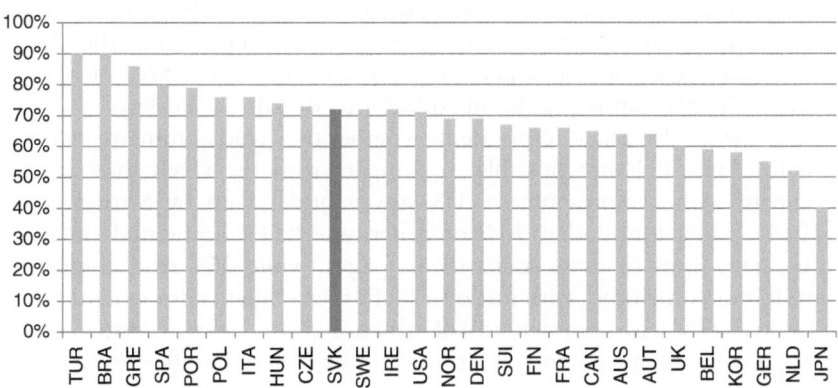

**Fig. 3.2** Participating in news. Sources as for Fig. 3.1.

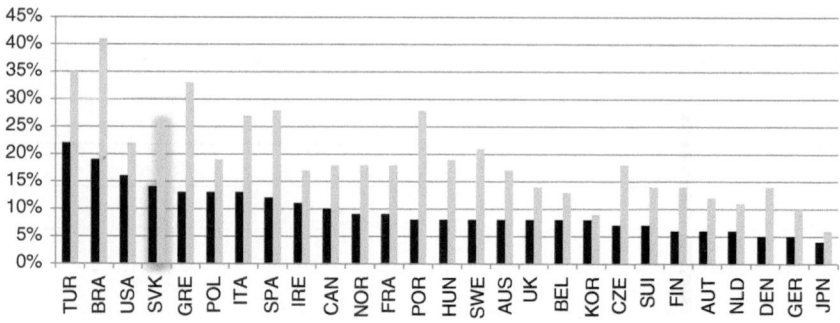

**Fig. 3.3**   Commenting on news Sources as for Fig. 3.1.

respondents said they usually did at least one of these things in an average week, less than the proportion in a number of southern European countries where news participation is particularly popular, but more than in most of western and northern Europe. In fact, there appears to be a Central European group of countries – Poland, Hungary, the Czech Republic and Slovakia – where participation is almost, but not quite as high as in southern Europe.

If we disaggregate these figures and focus specifically on commenting (Fig. 3.3), Slovakia stands out even more strongly as a place where people have developed a taste for having their say on the news, both via social media and on the websites of news organisations. For commenting on news websites, Slovakia is the leading country in the EU, behind only Turkey, Brazil and the USA among the countries included in the DNR. For commenting on social networks it is ahead of the USA but behind four Mediterranean EU states in addition to Brazil and Turkey.[5]

My survey also asked respondents whether they read comments to news articles. Here it is not possible to compare with the DNR, but we can compare with a representative US survey undertaken by Stroud et al. (2016). They found that 14% of Americans had commented on news sites, news apps or news social media pages, while 35% read comments but do not contribute, with just over half of respondents doing neither. In Slovakia, 27% had commented (of which 14% on news websites) while 50% said they read comments at least occasionally. The figure for those who read comments but do not contribute was correspondingly lower than the US case – 25% of the Slovak population are passive consumers of comments. However, I asked about commenting on social media in general, not just on news social media pages. The figure for those who read comments but do not comment directly on news websites is 37%, similar to the US results.

The demographics of news participation are interesting in several respects. If we compare Slovakia with the aggregated DNR results, the gender balance of different participatory news activities is not always the same. Internationally, while the overall picture of participation is balanced, men are more active commenters, especially on news websites, whereas slightly more women share news stories, especially on social networks. In Slovakia, even though the overall distribution of news participants is balanced, women are more inclined to participate than men when it comes to commenting both on websites and on social networks (where they also do more sharing). It is talking face-to-face about news which, in contrast to the international figures, is the most characteristic male activity in Slovakia.

As might be expected, participants are younger, more educated and wealthier than non-participants in news. The average age of those who participate in news, at 37, is eight years lower than the average age of all the respondents to the Slovak survey, and their average level of education and average income considerably higher – 24.5% of participants have a degree against 17.5% in the base sample, and 23.5% of participants have a monthly income above 1,500 EUR against 18% in the base sample. They are more or less representative, however, in terms of where they live: contrary to expectations, there is neither a significant over-representation of people from big cities and in particular the Bratislava region nor a significant under-representation of rural inhabitants among news participants. If, however, we compare different types of participation, there are notable differences between those who read and comment on news websites and those who read and comments on news on social networks. Those who are active on news websites are more educated and have higher incomes than those active on social networks, and among the former we get an over-representation of the capital together with an under-representation of villages with fewer than 2,000 inhabitants, whereas the social network commenters are more evenly geographically distributed.

Overall, there are thus grounds for arguing that Slovaks' news participation profile has some features that exaggerate trends observable throughout the world. It represents an extreme case (Flyvbjerg 2006), which may elucidate trends that would become more generalised if other countries were to see a continued increase in participation.[6] Slovakia, however, could also be called a critical case with regard to the development of online journalism and the market conditions of the national newspaper system. The small size of the market tends to makes competition for audiences more intense (Singer et al. 2011) and makes for chronic understaffing of newspapers. Furthermore Slovakia exhibits signs of strong economic and political heteronomy (the ability of economic and political interests to influence the media) for a variety of reasons, including the penetration of powerful financial groups into the ownership structure of most dailies, including *SME*, a phenomenon referred to locally as oligarchisation, and against which *Denník N* overtly positions itself. For both these reasons, Slovak newspapers are operating in an environment where it has become increasingly difficult not only to ensure editorial independence, but also to reproduce the resources necessary to sustain genres like investigative, immersive or contextual journalism (Fink and Schudson 2014), all forms to which the two case studies are strongly committed. Innovations that work in those conditions should be widely applicable.

## THE PROFESSION OF JOURNALISM IN SLOVAKIA

Since the collapse of the communist regime in 1989, the journalistic field in Central Europe has undergone significant structural transformations. The initial effect was to open the field to new entrants and bring in a period of post-revolutionary innovation and experimentation when 'journalistic practices and routines appear to have been guided more by civic than by professional values' (Metyková and Waschková Císařová 2009: 728), due to a high turnover of personnel and the foundation of many new titles, but also due to the engagement of journalists in the struggle to establish democratic institutions.

Throughout the 1990s most new entrants to the profession lacked journalistic training, since it was not until the middle of the decade that the first new journalism programmes were established in higher education institutions. This can be interpreted as an historical moment of refoundation, when a profession is temporarily amateurised by an influx of new entrants who challenge orthodox practices and values (severely compromised in this case by the higher-level political regime change) before the initially heretical values and practices become embedded as a new orthodoxy (Bourdieu 1998). In Slovakia this era was prolonged by the confrontational stance of the third Mečiar government (1994–1998) towards the media and other civil society institutions and the active participation of parts of the media, including *SME*, within a broad-based 'pro-democracy' campaign. Many of Slovakia's leading press titles were eventually bought by foreign publishing houses, but this trend has recently been reversed following retrenchments in the global media industry together with a growing interest by local financial groups in acquiring media brands. This is a worrying development given Waschková Císařová's earlier findings (2007) that direct pressure on journalists from proprietors had tended to decrease following foreign investment. A German publisher held a 50% stake in *SME* between 2000 and 2014, and it was the sale of this shareholding to a Slovak financial group, without a background in the press and implicated in a major political influence-buying scandal, that prompted a large part of the newsroom staff to leave and found *Denník N* as an 'independent' alternative.

As far as the profession of journalism is concerned, there are indications that it has been losing stability and prestige as an occupation. In Waschková Císařová's study (2007) some older journalists described a crisis in professional values and a decline in self-respect among members of the profession, citing, for example, a tendency for young people to join media organisations merely to make themselves visible so that they can move on to better-paid jobs, for example as spokespeople for economic or political organisations. Survey data also indicate that in 2010 around a third of Slovak journalists had considered leaving the profession, mainly for financial reasons, with only 23% of respondents convinced that they would continue to work in their current organisation (Brečka and Keklak 2010: 177–179). Although not the only cause, this instability is probably due partly to changes to workflows and job descriptions connected to newsroom digitalisation.

## Participation and Commenting at Case Study 1 – *SME*

The newspaper *SME* was founded in January 1993 when the Slovak government sacked the editor-in-chief of the state-owned newspaper *Smena*, by journalists who resigned in protest. Two years later the two papers merged, after *Smena* had been privatised. *SME* did not take very long to determine that first the Internet and later the social web represented market opportunities. It established a website in 1994 (initially in collaboration with a team from the Slovak Academy of Sciences), set up an online newsroom in 2000 and an in-house content management system the following year (using the know-how of Valér Kot, returning after postgraduate studies at the Université du Québec), enabled readers to comment on articles before any other Slovak newspaper, and was the second national newspaper in Europe to launch a blog platform for readers' blogs, in December 2004 (two weeks after *Le Monde* offered blogs to its subscribers). Its online news portal quickly established itself as the leading news portal in Slovakia, and was profit-making from 2005. *SME* has used participatory features as a key part of its business model, exploiting cultural capital that gave it a head start over most of its rivals.

Although many European newspapers initially experimented with a series of different participation channels (blogs, forums, polls and chats as well as interactive devices such as electoral candidate-matching tools), the trend has since been towards standardisation around a single format: comments below articles. In this respect, too, *SME* was slightly ahead of the global trend. According to Reich (2011: 98), Israel was one of the earliest adopters of comments to articles, in 2000. *SME* switched from forums to comments in 2004, at the same time as it launched its blog service, whereas it was not until the second half of the decade that the format became widespread and latterly almost universal. It nonetheless differs from most of its local competitors and international counterparts in the way it implements commenting through a range of different administration settings and associated practices. A given article can have one of four settings: pre-moderated, post-moderated, moderation delegated to author (for its 'VIP bloggers')[7] and closed to comments. Most, in fact, are post-moderated by four or five web editors in rotating shifts (see Chapter 4), but the fact that in certain respects the treatment of comments at *SME* has diversified over time is itself significant, because it goes against a general trend towards standardisation (Ihlebaek and Krumsvik 2015). In particular, the selective introduction of pre-moderation from January 2014 (mostly for articles on science and technology),[8] in an explicit attempt to improve discussion quality, goes against a trend for newspapers to switch from pre- to post-moderated discussion (Reich 2011). The mixed approach reflects continuing internal debates, uncertainties and experimentation with respect to how to calibrate this apparently standardised participation tool.

Compared with competing news portals in Slovakia, *SME*'s website does not give an especially prominent place to participation in terms of architecture and visibility, and does not offer features that are lacking on other portals, but it has the most extensive set of discussion rules and they are unique in offering a positive definition of what type of environment the newspaper wishes to create for its readers ('a place of intelligent debate') in addition to simply listing the negative forms of expression that are banned. *SME* aspires, in the words of its discussion codex,[9] to sustain 'a space for cultivated, substantive and non-aggressive communication between people for the purpose of familiarisation and opinion exchange'. Only two of the seven leading portals (*SME* and Topky) explain in their discussion rules how the alerting system works and encourage readers to use it, thereby indicating an intention to share the responsibility for discussion administration with readers (as will be described in greater detail in Chapter 4). *SME*'s rules are written in the first and second person (referring to the newspaper as 'we' and the user as 'you') where the norm is to adopt an impersonal third person register. This seems intended to introduce a conversational tone to the interaction between the medium and its online audience.

Although *SME*'s participatory offer to readers is now restricted to comments below articles, it is important, for a full understanding of its relationship to its online audience, to appreciate that it has an organisational culture marked by experiments in participatory journalism. Two personal anecdotes illustrate the point. In 2010, when I first made contact with the head of the then separate online division, *SME* had plans to recruit and support a network of hyperlocal bloggers. The ambition was to build on its highly successful blog platform and channel that energy into forms of citizen journalism that would complement professional journalism by focusing on neighbourhood-level issues. It was abandoned later, partly because of staff changes and partly because it was felt that the rise of social media had undercut the social demand and democratic value of such an initiative. The second example comes from my research: when I expressed an interest in looking at the effects on online discussion of engagement by journalists as authors, I found support from a deputy editor-in-chief and the head of online news, who nominated a few volunteers; we then ran five experimental 'author discussion' mornings, which I was able to observe. In this book I look at the involvement of journalist-authors in online discussion through the example of *Denník N*, where the practice was more systematised, but it is revealing, in view of the low status of admin work and the habitual dismissal of discussion's informational value by journalists, that *SME* was still interested in finding ways to do participation 'better' by reconfiguring the standard model.

## Participation and Commenting
## at Case Study 2 – Denník N

When, in late 2014, *SME*'s longest-serving editor-in-chief (2006–2014), all four of his deputies and around half the newsroom staff resigned in protest at the sale by the German co-owners of their 50% stake to a Slovak financial group whose political influence-peddling had in large part been brought to public attention by *SME*, it was natural that the new title they founded would commit itself to editorial independence. Framed in opposition to a narrative about the 'oligarchisation' of the Slovak media, the launch advertising campaign used two slogans: '*Denník N*,[10] a new independent newspaper' and 'no tabloid journalism, no oligarchs, no compromises'. N is hence a valuable site for studying the intensified boundary work that journalism currently faces (Carlson and Lewis (eds.) 2015), as it was born in an attempt to protect the boundary between the media and the economic and political spheres. Key to this goal was the ambition of building a strong subscriber base in order to be less reliant on income from advertising and support from institutional shareholders. This took time to achieve, but by late 2016 it could boast an operating surplus.

In many respects the founders sought to conserve or build on the positive legacy of *SME*, and one such area was participatory journalism. Without making it a plank of their launch publicity or their formal mission statements, participatory journalism was fundamental to their economic and cultural modus operandi. Firstly, during the autumn of 2014, when the website was operating on a shoestring budget and with very few staff (most resignees were serving out three months' notice at *SME*) blogs and bloggers gave the new site an important initial boost, since many bloggers from *SME* effectively joined the walkout and switched platforms out of solidarity. Secondly, social media played and continues to play an unusually significant role in driving traffic to the N website – Facebook, not Google, is the most important path into the website, generating around half of all visits. This in turn has an effect on the relative popularity of types of content: it is still not uncommon for a blog to be the most-read article on the entire site on a given day, an 'anomaly' attributed to the buzz that can be created by sharing links in Facebook circles.

But if blogs and social media were important for 'accidental' reasons connected to the origins and circumstances of the new medium (and perhaps to the very fact that it is a new medium), the management took a more programmatic stance with regard to discussion. Here they saw themselves as bearers of an ambivalent heritage from *SME*, where discussion had been phenomenally successful in quantitative terms, and contributed significantly to the portal's status as most used news portal in the country, but whose quality was perceived as having deteriorated over the years. This was not only a concern in itself (from the point of view of a desire to host a public debate worthy of the name), but also meant that administering discussion took up considerable human resources, something which N lacked. Technological factors also influenced the configuration of N's discussion system. Using a standard Wordpress content management system,[11] it lacked the technical means to manage large numbers of discussion contributions efficiently or the programming capacity to quickly create an inhouse solution equivalent to *SME*'s.

Instead N opted to try to set a new precedent for how comments facilities can be run. Thus its discussion system was introduced, at the time of the portal's official launch, with both an apology and a promise: discussion would be more selective than readers were used to at *SME* and other Slovak news portals, but journalists themselves would engage in online discussion beneath their articles.

> You won't find discussion below all the articles on the *Denník N* website. But where there are discussions, we'll be discussing too.
> ... They should be a place which neither you nor your children are afraid to enter. Where not only our readers can gather, but where we – the authors of articles, reporters, editors, newsroom managers – will be too. We'll be there so that we can respond to your questions, explain things that are unclear, or add details that you found missing in the article itself.
> (lead paragraph and extract from newsroom blog published on 5 January 2015)[12]

After a year and a half of operating, *Denník N* had yet to publish any discussion rules. In light of what was said earlier about *SME*'s discussion rules, one might assume that the absence of any codex indicates a neglect of discussion by *Denník N* and undermines its claim to offer a stronger participatory model to readers. The social media editor, who would have drafted the rules, had expected to have them ready within weeks of the launch, but three things prevented him from doing so: the fact that there was always something more urgent or important to do, the fact that he was not receiving complaints from participants about discussion administration, and the existence of a project for an in-house discussion system which was to replace the initial Wordpress plug-in. Since what goes in a codex is to some extent dependent on the technological affordances of the system, there was an obvious logic in waiting. But even when his project was postponed indefinitely due to the existence of higher programming priorities, the rules still never got written. Should we deduce from this that discussion is a low priority for the paper or that *Denník N* takes the purpose of having discussion rules seriously? As the social media editor explained, it would be simple to reproduce something similar to the codex he had known and used at *SME*, but he wanted to write something that 'reflects the changes that have happened on the Internet in the last five years' (such as the rise of political trolling of the type described in Chapter 6), and to reflect on 'whether we expect something else from contributors than was the case back then at SME' (interview 6.6.16). He summarised their position by specifying three functions that discussion rules should/would perform: a public manifesto about what the paper believes discussion should be like, a quasi-legal code which makes dispute resolution easier for both parties, and a codification of organisational knowledge 'for my eventual successor or for colleagues if we decided to share the administration workload more'.

In fact, the extent of role-sharing and boundary-blurring between traditional newsroom functions is already considerable at N and its empirical interest as a laboratory of emerging trends in journalistic work stems partly from this fact. Participatory functions are just one example of this. Partly due to its small size and low operating budget, N has a lean organisational structure, making do with virtually no specialist marketing staff, but instead exploiting the commercial knowledge of two members of the leadership on the reasoning that marketing has little short-term added value, whereas 'writing is our biggest asset' (interview with Head of Publishing 27.11.15). Similarly, it minimises the number of editors by asking reporters to be flexible and multi-skilled, taking care of aspects of the production of their articles such as page design and photo sourcing. Accordingly, N decided to devolve to authors chief responsibility for deciding whether to open discussions and (in theory at least) for monitoring and moderating them (see Chapter 5).[13] This adjustment of the socio-technical system for comments – a reallocation of roles within the newsroom and a promise of greater interaction between journalists and readers – made N a useful place to study an attempt to reconfigure the 'standard' model. In particular, their plans indicated to me that it would be interesting to track the work of regular journalists, since at N they assume a more prominent role in the ecology of online discussion than is common. Moreover, it was also a venue where organisational change could be studied in a live experiment, since my observations and interviews took place during the planning and the first year of operation of a new venture.

## A JOURNALISM OF OPINION OR COMMUNICATION?

One of this book's conceptual pillars is the idea that journalism can, like other modes of knowledge production such as science, be approached paradigmatically, if we understand a journalistic paradigm as a certain way of knowing or, more specifically, a set of conventions for producing 'news', that can change and has changed over the course of history, and which may also vary from one media system to another (Brin et al. 2004). Brin, Charron & de Bonville's hypothesis (published prior to the rise of social media and focusing on North American newspapers) was that print journalism is presently shifting gradually from an informational to a communicational paradigm (having previously known two other paradigms, which they call transmission and opinion). The names express the dominant trait of the four ages of journalism, but they are ideal types, and 'concrete paradigms' (the rules that journalists actually follow in a particular time and place) mix the functions of transmission, opinion, information and communication in different proportions. If we try, very schematically, to discern the conventions of the journalism practised at *SME* and *N* and map them onto Brin, Charron & de Bonville's typology, we see a pronounced hybridity. In some respects, the two papers, and the Slovak press in general, remain firmly wedded to the norm of objectivity championed by the journalism of information. Reporters on the main newsdesks tend to believe very strongly that it is important to report events factually and stay strictly neutral in relation to their sources and audiences (which is one factor that makes many of them reluctant to enter the discussion). But there are many familiar traits of what Brin, Charron & de Bonville call the *communicational* paradigm in the journalism practised by *SME* and *N*, especially in the generic choices and discursive techniques they use to facilitate the interpenetration of voices 'from below' with the news, whether through the large space they devote to lifestyle topics and other forms of 'soft news'[14] or the practice of 'sociological' journalism to represent points of view from civil society (focus groups, opinion surveys, field reports from 'typical' towns and villages). It is also evident in the employment of conversational, narrative or empathetic discursive styles – especially in the 'long-read' reportage format that both newspapers regularly devote space to – and in the stylistic and metadiscursive dimensions of journalists' prose, such as the diversity and creativity of introductory verbs in reported speech or the prominence given to scene-setting elements in a text: by introducing implicit evaluations of social actors' intentions and attitudes, or by making themselves present in the reported situation, journalists at both papers assume a more assertive discursive identity than they admit when declaring adherence to the objectivity norm.

But it is equally possible to argue that *SME* and *N* forged their reputations on a journalism that harks back to the journalism of *opinion* paradigm characteristic of the North American press in the nineteenth century, and which also corresponds more closely to Hallin and Mancini's (2004) Mediterranean model than to the North European or the Anglo-American types of media system.[15] It is a journalism that implicates newspapers as actors in political struggles, where they assume the right to accuse and denounce. Both papers are notably proactive in framing public problems, creating affairs, breaking scandals and adopting causes, initiating legal action or alerting authorities, advocating for institutional change, using investigative and campaigning journalism to introduce new issues (notably corruption) to the public sphere and perpetuating their visibility by returning to the same themes over extended periods (themes that may become the specialist 'dossiers' of particular reporters and commentators but which are claimed by the newspaper and attributed to it by other newspapers). As in other emerging democracies like Argentina, journalism has been an actor in democratic transition and consolidation (Boczkowski 2010: 181) and in accompanying struggles to define the institutional identity of the state.[16] It is a positioning that tends to be self-reproducing over time as it feeds off and fuels an antagonistic relationship with government, whose reprisal measures towards the press (from a history of legislative measures restricting press freedom to the repeated withdrawal of cooperation or accreditation from journalists perceived as 'oppositional' – exemplified by a systematic boycott of N by government ministers during 2015) make a collaborative stance more rather than less difficult for the opinion press.

The anchorage of a journalism of opinion in Slovak society is indicated by the very term that is most commonly used to describe the 'serious' or 'quality' press (the pole of the journalistic field with high symbolic capital): *mienkotvorný*, opinion-forming. The term implies an intention not only to inform (as in the journalism of information) or gratify (as in the journalism of communication) but also to persuade (Charron and De Bonville 2004: 189).

*Mienkotvorný* is a trope that often gets mobilised in the discussion as a legitimate model of journalism, as in the following exchange between a supporter and an opponent of *Denník N*'s line on a controversial topic:

Discussant 1:   [addressing journalist] You and I both know that *Denník N* had a clear position on the issue which it sought to promote both directly and indirectly. I was really supportive of your paper's launch but I expected journalism not an opinion-forming (*mienkotvorný*) newspaper...

Discussant 2:   I don't think that a quality newspaper can exist if it's not 'opinion-forming'

Discussant 1:   Naturally, it would have been better to write propagandistic than opinion-forming.

Discussant 1 is pulled up for 'misusing' the term as a negative qualifier and their concessionary reply indicates a shared assumption that it becomes a 'serious' newspaper to be opinion-forming as long as it stops short of 'propaganda'. I make clearer what the significance of opinion-forming journalism is for the things a newspaper can do with comments in Chapter 5, based on an analysis of polemical exchanges between journalists and members of the public.

## NOTES

1. For comparison with the potential market size, Slovakia's population is around 5.4 million, and roughly 2 million more Slovak-speakers live abroad.

2. http://www.digitalnewsreport.org/survey/2016/further-analysis-2016/ [accessed 9.7.16].

3. The survey I commissioned was a classical door-to-door survey, while the DNR is an online survey using a weighted sample to ensure representativeness with respect to standard demographic and socio-economic indicators. Given the different collection methods it is debatable whether it is best to express my results as percentages of the total sample or the Internet-using part of the sample (approximately 70%). Neither solution is ideal. The former would underestimate the prevalence of online activities in Slovakia, while the latter would overestimate them given that the Slovak online sub-sample is over-educated and younger in comparison with the total population. I have opted to take the conservative position and compare my results for the total population with the percentages reported in the DNR. Even so,

the figures for Slovakia are close to the digitally active/participative end of the spectrum, which makes the findings all the more impressive.

4.  Respondents were prompted with examples: the UK version of the DNR gave BBC News, Mail Online and the Huffington Post as examples; the Slovak questionnaire gave the four most popular news portals in the country – sme.sk, cas.sk, topky.sk and aktuality.sk.

5.  The Brazilian and Turkish samples in the DNR are only representative of urban populations.

6.  DNR evidence is actually equivocal here – some countries see continued increases in participation while others have seen a tailing off in recent years.

7.  VIP bloggers are accorded greater visibility on the main blog page (and also by the very fact that they can be viewed as a separate list) as well as being allowed to administrate the discussion beneath their own articles.

8.  The topic choice was driven by two factors: a sense that it was legitimate and realistic to impose more exigent standards of 'intelligent debate'; and, crucially, the willingness of science journalists to do the moderation (unlike post-moderated debate, pre-moderation is not usually left to the regular admin team).

9.  http://www.sme.sk/diskusie/kodex/ [accessed 8.7.16].

10. Denník means 'daily newspaper', and the mysterious letter N could also stand for newspaper (*noviny*), but is more likely to evoke the Slovak word for independent (*nezávislý*). The paper is often just called N for short.

11. In January 2016 (after the end of my fieldwork) it switched to a Facebook plugin, largely to reduce the workload of administration.

12. https://dennikn.sk/blog/preco-nie-je-diskusia-pod-vsetkymi-clankami/ [accessed 8.7.16].

13. At N web editors play an important role in the selection of articles for discussion but do not perform administration shifts like they do at *SME*. The social media editor, however, plays an essential 'backstop' role both in monitoring open discussions and in communicating with participants.

14. Soft news is heavily represented in my corpus of discussion threads in which journalists at N actually participated (see Chapter 5): 28% of these articles were classifiable as soft news during the first half of 2015.

15. Given that the pattern of news participation in Slovakia, according to the survey results reported previously, also has a southern European flavour, it is tempting to suggest that we see here a certain adjustment between journalistic discourse and audience behaviour.

16. At several points in Slovakia's post-communist history, freedom of expression has been perceived as under threat, which is reflected in the country's oscillating ranking in international indices – in 2004 *Reporters sans frontières* ranked Slovakia top its World Press Freedom Index, but by 2009 it had slipped as low as 44th place (following new 'right of reply' legislation widely seen as punitive), before rising back to 12th in 2016.

## REFERENCES

Boczkowski, P. (2010). *News at work: Imitation in an age of information abundance*. Chicago: Chicago University Press.

Bourdieu, P. (1998). *Les règles de l'art. Genèse et structure du champ littéraire*. Paris: Seuil.

Brečka, S., & Keklak, R. (2010). Novinárska profesia na Slovensku 2010. In S. Brečka, B. Ondrášik, & R. Keklak (Eds.) *Média a novinári na Slovensku 2010* (pp. 121–210). Bratislava: Eurokódex.

Brin, C., Charron, J., & De Bonville, J. (2004). *Nature et transformation du journalisme. Théorie et recherches empiriques*. Laval (Québec): Les presses de l'université Laval.

Carlson, M., & Lewis, S. (Eds.) (2015). *Boundaries of journalism: Professionalism, practices and participation*. Abingdon & New York: Routledge.

Charron, J., & De Bonville, J. (2004). Typologie historique des pratiques journalistiques. In C. Brin, J. Charron, & J. De Bonville (Eds.) *Nature et transformation du journalisme. Théorie et recherches empiriques* (pp. 141–218). Laval (Québec): Les presses de l'université Laval.

Fink, K., & Schudson, M. (2014). The rise of contextual journalism, 1950s–2000s. *Journalism, 15*(1), 3–20.

Flyvbjerg, B. (2006). Five misunderstandings about case-study research. *Qualitative Inquiry, 12*, 219–245.

Hallin, D., & Mancini, P. (2004). *Comparing media systems: Three models of media and politics*. Cambridge: Cambridge University Press.

Ihlebaek, K., & Krumsvik, A. (2015). Editorial power and public participation in online newspapers. *Journalism, 16*(4), 470–487.

Metyková, M., & Waschková Císařová, L. (2009) Changing journalistic practices in Eastern Europe. The cases of the Czech Republic, Hungary and Slovakia. *Journalism, 10*(5), 719–736.

Reich, Z. (2011). User comments: The transformation of participatory space. In J. Singer et al. (Eds.), *Participatory journalism. Guarding open gates at online newspapers* (pp. 96–117). Malden, MA & Oxford: Wiley-Blackwell.

Singer, J., Hermida, A., Domingo, D., Heinonen, A., Paulussen, S., Quandt, T., Reich, Z., & Vujnovic, M. (2011). *Participatory journalism. Guarding open gates at online newspapers*. Malden, MA and Oxford: Wiley-Blackwell.

Stroud, N., Van Duyn, E., & Peacock, C. (2016). *News commenters and news comment readers*. Engaging News Project report. Available at: https://engagingnewsproject.org/enp_prod/wp-content/uploads/2016/03/ENP-News-Commenters-and-Comment-Readers1.pdf [accessed 9.7.16].

Waschková Císařová, L. (2007). *Report on news cultures in Slovakia*. EMEDIATE Project, WP3 National Report, unpublished report.

# CHAPTER 4

# Judging the Quality of Online Discussion: The Invisible Work of 'Admins'

**Abstract** Smith describes the work routines of discussion administrators over the first 12 years of online commenting at a Slovak daily newspaper, detailing who has done the job, how the technological equipment has changed, and how admins make and justify judgements. Changes in the workforce and interface redesigns have distanced moderation work from the discussion milieu in an attempt to professionalise and routinise it. When observed up close, however, admins' cognitive work and enacted competences are less classificatory and more inferential than one would expect for a role at the low end of the intraprofessional status hierarchy. Like other front-line professionals, discretionary space and hesitation are essential both to deal with human complexity and to retain a sense of professionalism.

**Keywords** Admin · Discussion administration · Interface · Moderator · Professional discretion · Professional inference

This chapter describes the constitution and performance of a routine on the fringes of journalism – the work of online discussion administrators (or 'admins'). In order to explore the influence of factors such as staff turnover, division of labour and technological design over a relatively long period and within a relatively stable organisational setting, it uses historical and observational data on the organisation of

© The Author(s) 2017
S. Smith, *Discussing the News*, Palgrave Studies in Science,
Knowledge and Policy, DOI 10.1007/978-3-319-52965-3_4

discussion admi nistration during the first 12 years of news comment-ing at the older case study, *SME*. The historical period is reconstructed based on interviews with six former administrators (who worked at *SME* during the period 2004–2013) and with the programmer who designed the technological interface that administrators used between 2009 and 2015. The twin purpose of these interviews was to obtain a retrospective account of how ex-admins remember the task being performed in the past and to produce biographical narratives in order to understand how admin work fitted into journalistic trajectories and professional identities. In 2013–2014, five administrators were observed at work, using a think-aloud protocol, in order to understand both how they interacted with the technology and how they justified their decisions to approve or delete comments. This exercise was repeated in 2016 following a complete staff turnover and a major interface redesign, in order to observe the influence of these factors on task performance, and so help understand the impact of managerial policies and of workplace organisation.

## THE CONSTRAINING AND ENABLING EFFECTS OF ROUTINES

While there is an abundance of research dealing with the deliberative quality of online news comments, which tends either to assess quality against a Habermasian ideal speech situation (e.g. Misnikov 2010, Ruiz et al. 2011), or to relate comment quality to participant motivation (e.g. Mitchelstein 2011; Diakopoulos and Naaman 2011), comparatively few studies describe commenting policies (e.g. Robinson 2010) and fewer still look at how comment administration is organised and performed as a cognitive work routine. Notable exceptions are Ihlebaek and Krumsvik (2015) and Degand (2012), and only Degand used ethnographic methods. This is surprising given the long tradition of studying journalism from a sociology of work perspective and the well established genre of newsroom ethnography, which Paterson and Domingo (2008) urged researchers of online news production to engage with. My point of departure is a similar research question to Ihlebaek & Krumsvik's – 'how is editorial control practised in partici-patory services in online newspapers?' (2015: 471) – but turns it much more closely towards situated practice than their survey was able to do. I aim to describe the competences enacted by admins, including how they are materialised by technological arrangements and scripted by the institutions that structure the organisational and professional field. The chapter problematises common assumptions both about the relationship of the new skills required to facilitate eParticipation to the traditional skillset of professional journalists and about the relationship of the participatory competences that administrators pass judgement on to the critical competences they enact as judges. Admin work requires a specific set of competences that differ in important ways from the editorial skills prioritised in journalism, which resemble even less the skills and dispositions associated with the figure of the 'community manager', but which can still be described as highly 'professional' if by that we mean the maintenance of a dynamic balance between classificatory and inferential reasoning in the accomplishment of work tasks (Abbott 1988). When we take a diachronic view – considering how the organisation of discussion administration has evolved over the 12 years since comments below articles were launched – there is nonetheless a tension between professionalising and deprofessionalising trends.

The rest of the chapter is divided into three sections that tell the story of how admining at *SME* has evolved from different perspectives: an account of who does the job, an account of its technological equipment, and an account of how admins make and justify judgements.

## Who Does the Job? Defining the Right Bundle of Tasks

Newspapers and news portals that facilitate readers' comments have different kinds of arrangements for ensuring their administration or moderation.[1] In some cases it is sub-contracted to a third-party service provider, in some cases volunteers are recruited among the readers or 'community members', and where it is handled within the newsroom it may be entrusted to people specifically employed for that task (often called community managers) or delegated to members of the journalistic staff as one of their responsibilities. *SME* has eventually settled on the latter model, but not before it had experimented with different ones.

Figure 4.1 shows the changing composition of the main admin workforce.[2] The periodisation divides quite neatly into three eras: the pioneering

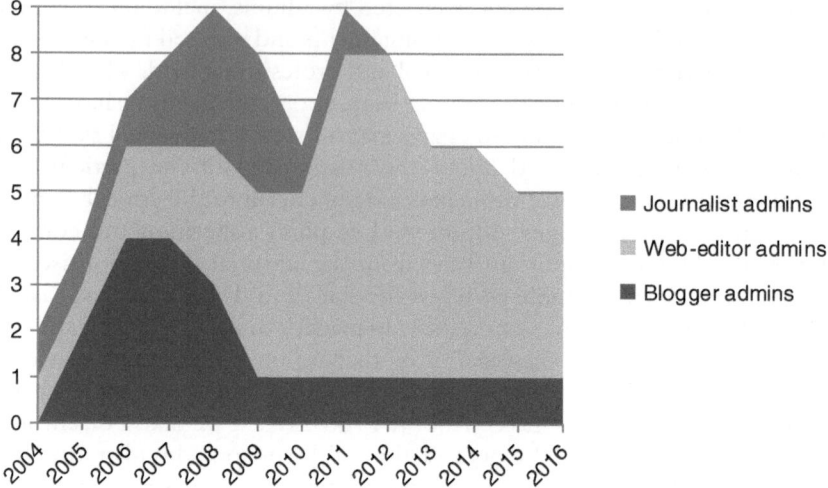

**Fig. 4.1** Composition of the admin workforce

first two years, when there were only two admins (one a journalist specialising in computers, the other the night-duty editor who singlehandedly put the newspaper online in those days); a four-year period when the bulk of admins were co-opted from among *SME*'s VIP bloggers (effectively outsourcing the task to a trusted segment of the 'community');[3] and the post-2010 period, when discussion administration was more or less formally included in the web-editor's bundle of tasks (though not until 2015 was it actually listed in their job descriptions). It also shows that during the transitional period (2008–2010) two or three journalists regularly deleted or approved comments. This does not mean that it was part of their regular job – the only journalist who had regular admin shifts was the computer reporter (later a deputy editor-in-chief) who founded most of *SME*'s participatory services. But in those years two other deputy editors-in-chief intervened occasionally, usually following complaints or when an alert was referred upwards by the on-duty admin. Their involvement is an indication of 'customer relations' problems, problems with keeping the discussion in order, or hesitation and uncertainty in the application of the rules. This was in fact one of the motivations for confining discussion administration to the newsroom. The transition period also coincides with the three years in which *SME* operated a separate online division, located one floor above the main newsroom.[4] In this section I describe the significant characteristics of the 'typical admin' during each period based on data collected from 16 of the roughly 20 people who have done the task.[5]

### The Pioneers

Roundabout 2004 they increased my hours to do the news releases at night. I used to finish putting the paper online around midnight, and they had a gap between 10 pm and 6am when no one was processing the news agency stuff. And administrating the discussion just really belonged to that role – whoever had the agency shift dealt with the discussion as well. (Web-editor admin, 2004–2008)

The first two discussion administrators, following the launch of comments below articles in 2004, were the reporter who edited a computers supplement (later head of the temporarily separate online division, and still later a deputy editor-in-chief) and the person whose job it was to transfer articles from the newspaper onto the web. As in most newspapers at the time, this was a manual operation performed in the late evening. Starting with the same articles that had just gone to press, he would make some basic typographic and layout alterations, correct any mistakes he spotted, and publish them online. Working from home, he usually finished around midnight. Someone had the idea that it would be useful to have him monitor agency news releases at night, when the newsroom was empty and he accepted an offer to cover what would essentially become the web-editing role through the early hours of the morning. Discussion was added onto this bundle for similar reasons of complementarity: the computers reporter only took care of administration during the working day, so someone on an evening shift was the perfect match. It is symptomatic of the whole history of discussion administration that the person appointed to do it was not chosen because they had particular skills or dispositions that were thought to suit the job, but because they were available, or because there was a synergy with something else they did. The second admin, indeed, was seen by others as someone typologically unsuited to discussion administration:

He was temperamentally a classical discussant, not an admin. A frustrated person, combustible. But no one else knew the system, they needed him to put the paper online. (Web-editor admin, 2008–2010)

Little has changed there: web-editors are not taken off the job if it transpires that they have aptitudes that do not suit administration and collegial advice within the team of web-editors is the only correction mechanism. In one respect, though, this era was unique: both administrators routinely intervened in the discussion to explain their decisions (in fact they acted almost like moderators). With hindsight, both regard this as a mistake, particularly the 'combustible' web-editor, who frequently got into extended arguments:

> I tried to explain why and how something had been deleted. If someone is convinced that their contribution is fine and appropriate, then you don't stand a chance of getting your point across. Maybe the victims appreciated it – yes, I think those we stuck up for were grateful. But as soon as you start to discuss with 'them', you give them an easy target: I became the lightning rod for their attacks. (Web-editor admin, 2004–2008)

Interventions by admins in the discussion have declined through each of the three eras, and only one of the nine admins observed in 2013–2014 and 2016 was a regular discussion participant.

### *The Blogger Admins*

During 12 years of comments below articles at *SME*, the 'something else' to which admining has been bolted on has not always been the web-editor role. For about four years it was more often appended to the role of blogger.

> The chief blog administrator had a great idea – employ bloggers, the better ones, whom you knew you could rely on, to look after the discussion [under blogs], so that the community would take care of its own needs. And then he looked among them for suitable people to administrate the discussion to news articles as well. (Web-editor admin, 2009–2013)

Hence four of the admins between 2006 and 2009 were readers who had started blogs on the *SME* portal, had become active in the blogging 'community' and had then been approached by *SME*'s blog administrator (himself a 'graduate' from blogging, without a journalistic background) to join an elite group of bloggers who, for a small fee, provide a technical support service to new bloggers and in addition administrate the discussion beneath blogs. Since the discussion system for blogs and news is technologically identical and interconnected, they were seen as ideal candidates to become general discussion administrators: 'often there was a progression: blogger – VIP blogger – blog admin – discussion admin' (Journalist admin, 2004–2010). For a two-year period, indeed, one of these blogger admins took overall charge of discussion administration, on a sub-contractual basis, working from home. While he shared duties with web-editors in the newsroom (whom he never met) he says he more or less worked non-stop:

> I got a flat fee, but I'm a person who does something 200% if I'm going to take it on, and since I would be at the computer for 20 hours a day [mostly doing translating and correcting work] I could do the discussion 'with one eye' alongside my normal work. I did that for two years and then I'd had enough – it was quite nerve-racking [referring both to his workload and to the psychological strains of interacting with discussants]. (Blogger admin, 2008–2009)

Even his case, however, conforms to the rule that someone's capacity and availability for the task is discovered opportunistically – that discussion administration is the addition to a portfolio of other tasks or concerns. He approached *SME* in his capacity as a corrector, aghast at the frequency of typographical and grammatical errors he came across. *SME* took up his offer to act as a sort of additional, freelance copy editor, and then:

> One thing led to another. The technological system fascinated me, they made me a blog admin, and then they asked me if I wouldn't take on administration of the discussions as well. (Blogger admin, 2008–2009)

### The Web-editor Admins

The arrangement that prevailed from 2009 onwards – the integration of administration within the web-editor role – coincides with the dissolution of the separate online division and reflected the gradual establishment of the web-editor role as something no longer experimental but a stable and important part of newsroom work. Managers say they observed a synergy with discussion administration based on the assumption that it is an advantage to have a good overview of the stories on the home page and their popularity. Since the on-duty web-editor constantly monitors audience figures in order to make decisions about the positioning of stories on the home page, and since they read and edit many of those stories, they were seen as ideally suited for the task.[6] But reintegration was partly also a response to what the deputy editor-in-chief called 'a heap of problems': a perceived need to achieve more consistency in how the rules of discussion were interpreted in the face of mounting complaints from participants in a conscious attempt at standardisation and systematisation. Admins who witnessed this transition speak of a process of professionalisation, contrasted with an 'amateurish' lack of planning hitherto. Nevertheless, professionalisation only extended to personnel decisions – to the assignment and organisation of work. It did not extend to training, monitoring and evaluation, which all continued to be handled informally through on-the-job learning and peer advice. What the term professionalisation captures is how the job has been fully absorbed within a journalistic bundle of tasks and assigned to people who invariably have a journalistic eduction and think of themselves as journalists. This mode of integration corresponds to what Abbott calls *career-based task degradation* – assigning 'dirty work' that no one really wants to do to novices, on the tacit understanding that it is a temporary assignment, a sort of initiation ritual. According to Abbott (1988: 126), this is a common way for professions to keep control of undignified tasks on their margins but which they still regard as important because it affects either the inputs to (dignified) professional work or the public image of the profession.

The changing way in which work was assigned and organised led to a radical change in the profile of those who did it: All nine web-editors observed at work between 2013 and 2016 were graduates of Slovak or Czech universities in journalism or media studies. For about half of them, *SME* was their first job since graduation, whilst the others had worked briefly at another newspaper or news portal before joining *SME*. The five who left *SME* all remained in the media (four transferring to N, one moving into the press office of a political institution). This background contrasts with the profile of their predecessors: out of about 10 administrators whom *SME* employed from 2004 to 2009, six had studied humanities or social science subjects and only one studied journalism. Furthermore, their previous and subsequent jobs were more often in the software, new media or creative industries than in journalism.

'Professionalisation' has thus ensured that the people doing the job have a journalistic practical sense. This helps the web-editor admin form a relatively clear and consistent image of the model discussant to news, since this figure is the counterpart of a familiar speaker – the reporter, the editorialist or the newspaper as a discursive subject. But, as current and former web-editor admins candidly admitted, the blogger admins had a better feel for the mood of the blog 'community':

> I was most uncertain with [comments to] blogs. I didn't get that community. Its jibes. I wasn't one of them, like X and Y [two of his contemporary blogger admins]. It was a kind of caste system. Often I didn't want to intervene. (Web-editor admin, 2008–2010)

There are some grounds for believing that this problem might extend beyond the specific case of discussion to blogs. Professionalisation has led to a more or less deliberate distanciation from the discussion as milieu. Disinterest is equated with neutrality and objectivity.[7] As we will see in the following sections, the routines and interfaces that mediate the task of discussion administration are implicated in this process of distanciation, and sometimes the shortcuts they offer are deliberately circumvented. Equipped with tools designed to isolate and streamline the act of judgement by eliminating 'superfluous' textual information, the admin frequently does a good deal of intertextual reconstruction work to reattach comments both to the discussion milieu and to journalism itself.

## What Tools are Used? Designing the Right Interface

Although in theory and in terms of legal responsibility newspapers should monitor entire discussions, in practice admins rarely have time even to scan the discussion below articles (which can quickly expand to hundreds of contributions spread over dozens of pages). Their principal working interface is a list, appearing in reverse chronological order, called the 'admin notice list' or 'list of alerts'. Admins react to alerts received from discussion participants, who pressed a button 'Alert the administrator'. The on-duty administrator has to decide if the complaint is valid – and the comment should be 'blocked' – or invalid – and the comment left in place. This section details the evolution of the interface

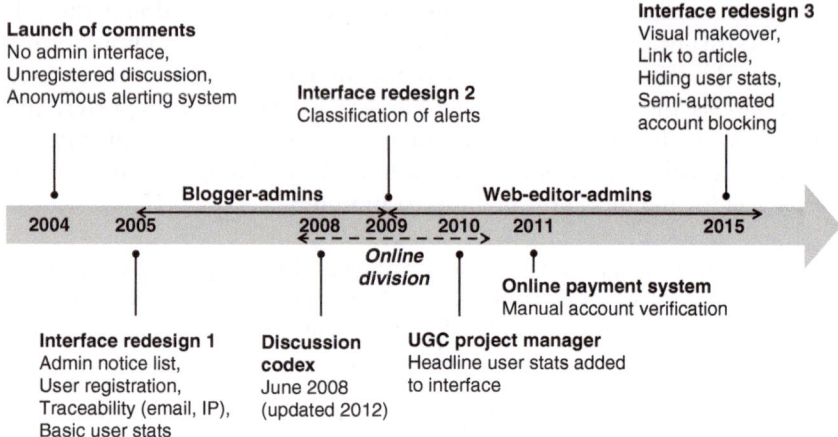

**Fig. 4.2**   Timeline of personnel, organisational and interface design changes

for handling alerts and its appropriation by admins as a working tool. It has evolved through three main redesigns (see Fig. 4.2). Figures 4.3 and 4.4 show the look of the 2009–2015 and post-2015 interfaces, respectively. A screenshot of the original interface could not be found.

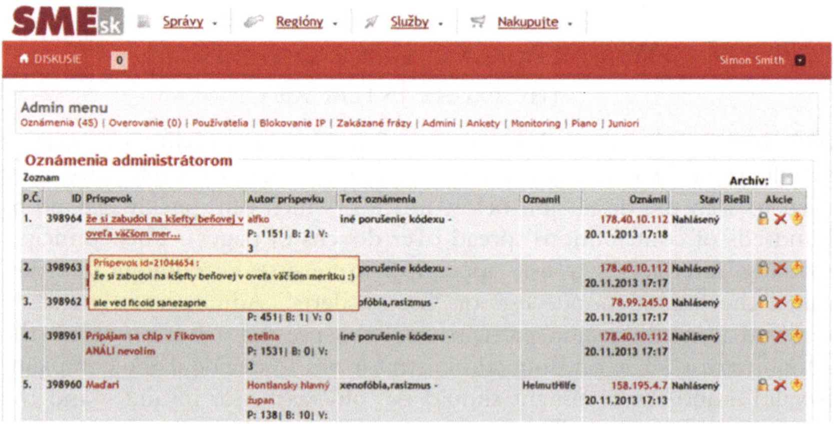

**Fig. 4.3**   Admin notice list, 2009–2015. Reproduced with permission from *SME*

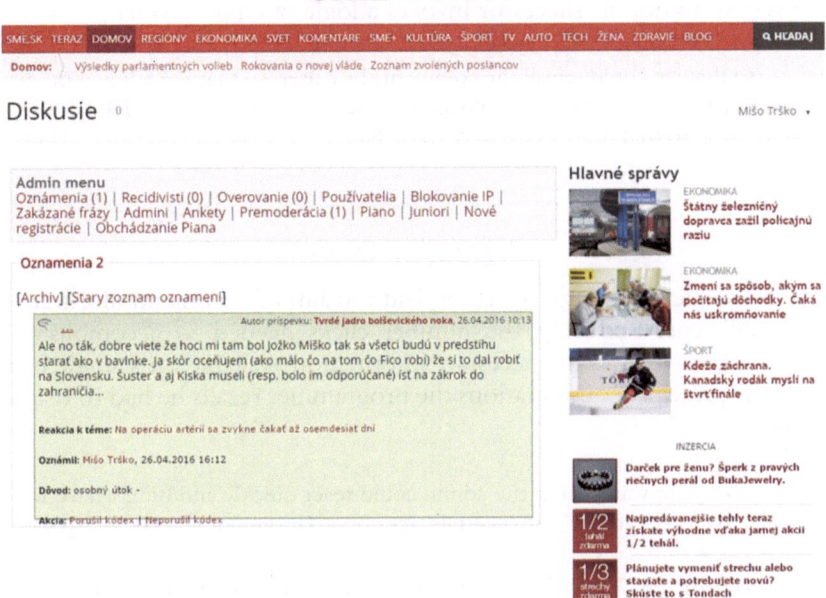

**Fig. 4.4**  Admin notice list, 2015–2016. Reproduced with permission from *SME*

## The System of Alerts

At the very beginning, according to the two original admins, there was no registration system for discussion: 'you just entered a nickname and wrote your contribution' (Web-editor admin, 2004–2008). A system of alerting already existed, but on receiving an alert the admin had to open the discussion, find the reported comment and then decide whether to leave it or delete it, 'although it seemed like you had more time then, so it wasn't a problem', the original journalist admin (2004–2010) recalls. User registration was introduced in 2005 together with the original 'admin notice list'. In the recollection of the first web-editor admin, the system was reprogrammed on the direct order of the editor-in-chief, alarmed that one of the paper's guest columnists had threatened to stop writing for *SME* if they did not do something about vulgarity and personal attacks in the comments. The programmer got a commission to create a system that would be 'administrate-able'. When describing what management wanted the system to do, his successor invokes a logic of empowerment:

> ... so that we could see all the comments by a user, so that the admin could see IP addresses, so that he could alter usernames, so that he could see email addresses, so that individuals were traceable ... (Programmer, 2007–2014)

### Reputation Control

The subsequent redesign, in 2009, had the aim of making administration more efficient. Reducing the number clicks needed to accomplish an action and having all the necessary information available on a single page were the principal considerations the programmer recalls he had to bear in mind:

> The basic aim was so that the admin could react quickly and didn't have to make five clicks to perform a certain action... (Programmer, 2007–2014)

Column 5 in the 2009–2015 interface shows the first main innovation of this redesign: the alert's classification. A few months previously the newly established online division had composed and published a discussion codex, which detailed, among other rules, four main categories of offence for which comments would be deleted: vulgarity, personal attack, xenophobia/racism and advertising/spam. As noted in Chapter 3, the codex is unusual among Slovakia's main news portals in explicitly encouraging readers to use the alerting system, indicating an intention to share the responsibility for discussion administration with readers. This allowed the alerting system to be simplified: instead of asking for an individual justification, the user was prompted to tick one of the four categories (or an 'other' category) with the option (infrequently used) of adding an explanation:

> ... so that the admin didn't have a lot of superfluous text. Because as you can see [we were looking at the archive of alerts], most people don't want to write anything .... (Programmer, 2007–2014)

The other main innovations that the 2009–2015 interface brought were concerned with reputation control. Three of the columns provide identifying indicators for both the alerter and the 'accused'. In columns 6 and 7 (see Fig. 4.3) are the username of the alerter (not shown if the alert was sent anonymously) and the IP address from which the alert was sent. These data serve principally to make visible a series of alerts by the same user, which tends to reduce their credibility for an admin. In column 4, meanwhile, we see the accused's username and three numbers that serve as reputational indicators: the total number of comments by the user (P), the number of deleted comments (B) and the number of warnings sent to that user by an admin (V). The 'PBV' figures were added to the interface shortly after its inception at the suggestion of the person who was appointed project manager for user-generated content (UGC) in 2010, 'so that the admin knew straight away who they're dealing with' (programmer, 2007–2014). *SME* has not gone as far as some newspapers that have created hierarchical systems of user rights based on reputation management,[8] but making the data visible for the admin encouraged the latter to adopt them as orientational indicators. Admins often referred to these figures in their justifications when I observed them in 2013–2014.

In order to make room for some of the new data which the programmer had been asked to include on the interface, however, the actual wording of the comment had to be hidden from immediate view. When I asked the programmer about this, he explained:

> There could be more information there, you could add an extra column, but it would be uncomfortable. That's why I used that pop-up bubble [for the actual comment], because it wouldn't fit on the screen if you had it as a separate column. (Programmer, 2007–2014)

Although during observation admins always looked at the comment, first by hovering the mouse over its title (the red underlined text in column 3), and then sometimes by clicking on it (which takes them into the discussion), the first things they saw before making a judgement were quantified details about the communicating subject, not the text of the communication. In the latest interface redesign, however, this prioritisation was reversed.

### *Partial Automation of the Admin Routine*

In 2015 the interface was once again redesigned (see Fig. 4.4). The most obvious change was a visual makeover which mimics the look of the discussion threads. It also restores to the centre of the admin's visual perspective the actual message of the reported comment, while at the same time hiding from view all of the identifying indicators apart from the two usernames. To find out IP addresses and reputational indicators an admin now has to click on one of these. The ostensive effect is to nudge them towards a judgement based on the content of the reported comment. However the logic for the change lies less in any conscious effort to 'judge the message not the messenger' than in a horizontal division of labour that takes the process of routinising admin work one step further.

As with many of the other changes, there was more contingency than planning in this task delegation. One of the tasks assumed by the UGC project manager was to manually verify new user accounts. The need to do so came from an attempt to encourage people to discuss under their real names, by giving them the option of including in their signature a link to their blogs and/or photo albums elsewhere on the *SME* portal. From 2011 he also took on the job of tracking multiple accounts suspected of having been set up to get round the new online payment system (which limits non-subscribers to three comments per day). The third interface redesign extends this logic, fixing a horizontal division of labour in which admins deal with comments, while users and their reputations are the business of the UGC project manager. It is a division of labour based on specialisation rather than escalation (there is no routine of referral and no distinction in user rights), and the way that admins often described their competences to me in interview was to refer to the tab at the top of the admin notice list which they regarded as 'their business': the *Oznámenia* tab, or the list of alerts. Most of the other tabs (the red labels under the heading *Admin menu* on Fig. 4.4) 'belong' to the UGC project manager, and most deal in users, notably the *Recidivisti* tab (a list of 'repeat offenders' which enables accounts to be blocked or warnings sent), the *Overovanie* tab (for verifying new nicknames and links to blogs) and the *Nové registrácie* and *Obchádzanie Piana* tabs (for new registrations and for detecting subversions of the online payment system).

So far, this all applies to the situation before 2015 as well – the new interface just 'ratifies' a division of labour that had emerged slowly as *SME* reconfigured its participatory services. But a second innovation in 2015 was an attempt to automate more of the admin work. Specifically, the decision to block a user's account has been part-automated. Five blocked comments within 30 days now results in a blocked account, unless overridden by the UGC project manager, who explained:

> Exceptions usually get made if the discussant appeals – I start to look more closely at how they discuss, whether they deserve it. If it really matters to a discussant to remain in this community, they have to do something extra (i.e. write to us and explain their comments). (email communication with UGC project manager no. 2, 2016)[9]

As we will see in the next section, looking at the way someone discusses over time is something which admins themselves quite often do. But in order to do so they have to dig beneath the immediate options the interface offers, working around the affordances of their basic tool and doing something that overlaps with the UGC project manager's routine. So while the disappearance of the 'PBV' data from the new interface is in one sense just the logical result of the more complex division of labour between editors, managers and machines, the reality of everyday admin work, deleting and passing comments on the news, requires its restoration. In fact, neither the new interface that nudges admins towards the quality control of text nor the older one that nudged them towards the reputational control of users based on simple indicators provides adequate contextual information for a good half of the 'cases' they judge. Instead, the roles they need to perform to feel they are doing a professional job oblige them to find workarounds to the standard procedures inscribed in their tools.

## WHAT ROLES ARE PERFORMED? ADMINS' JUSTIFICATORY VOCABULARY

> Norms and procedure are their expertise; hesitation is their duty (Weller 2012: 18)

The core of an admin's job is to pass judgements about comments that are accused of having broken the discussion rules. They interpret and apply those rules. How do they do so, and what competences do they need? How are judgements affected by who does the job and the tools they have? Ethnographic methods are ideally suited to answering these kinds of questions, so it would be dangerous to attempt a description of the *former* admins' judgemental and decision-making work on the basis of retrospective interviews, but I still have the ability to compare two points in time, separated by three years, a major interface redesign and a wholesale staff turnover. This section rests on my newsroom observation work, which employed a method developed to overcome a problem encountered in the early stages of fieldwork. When observing online discussion administration being performed, there were no clearly marked contextual clues about how to interpret what was going on. Job descriptions, official organisational procedures, training manuals and legal codes would have been the natural yardsticks, but these scarcely exist. Discussion administration is a social practice without any codified scripts at *SME*. But, in order to do the job efficiently, admins nevertheless did what members of organisational groups do in a variety of routine situations – they typified, referring to categories (Sumpter 2000). This meant that it was possible to use research situations to produce textual artefacts that invoked a normative context equivalent to the missing standards. Instead of silently observing, I prompted administrators to justify each decision that they took, including the doubts and self-questioning that preceded judgements (Weller 2011), recording the qualifying words and phrases that they used. The result of this exercise was a series of texts in the form of lists of adjectival words and phrases. Adjectives attribute qualities to entities and thus singularise them by referring to a local context within which the attributions apply, or by defining legitimate and illegitimate comparisons with other contexts (Chateauraynaud 2003: 231). They referred me to the discursive registers that seemed relevant to individuals at a particular time and place. They invoked a series of standards, norms and categories that oriented their judgement, including organisational policies and values as well as internalised, socialised thresholds of quality.

My methodological claim, in line with Weller's approach to studying the invisible deliberative work of magistrates, is that the internal dialogues that accompany individual judgemental work are often better graspable through studying documents – in this case externalised verbalisations recorded by the researcher – than the usual alternative of retrospective interviews (Weller 2011). This is the logic of a 'think-aloud protocol' (Ericsson and Simon 1993): that my observation would produce texts – my observation notes of administrators' actions and decisions – which literally contained their own contexts – the externalised justifications produced in response to my questioning. The subsequent analytical task was then to ascertain what registers these justifications referred to, since this is crucial to understanding what kind of legitimacy administrators claim when judging online discussion. This proceeded through several rounds of coding, until my codes eventually converged around six categories that mapped onto Abbott's distinction between two basic types of reasoning in professional knowledge practices: classification and inference. This distinction is important for Abbott because it tends to correspond closely to a status division within professional groups between more or less noble work. Formal inferential work has higher status, but the two sets of tasks are interdependent: a profession that accomplished only inferential work could not maintain public legitimacy, for which the existence of relatively stable and acceptable categories is essential.[10]

One can say that professionals infer in those situations when they have considerable discretionary space, and they classify when this space closes. Less tautologically, professionals claim discretionary space when classifications fail them and they 'need' to infer. Wallander and Molander (2014) argue that it is more accurate to see a continuum in the degree of discretion a professional worker has, depending upon how strong the warrants are (the 'norms of action') in different working situations. That would imply that the balance between classification and inference might also be a matter of 'more/less' rather than 'either/or' – a matter of the size of the intuitive gap that needs bridging to move from an antecedent to its consequent during what Abbott calls diagnostic or treatment decisions. My coding scheme is an attempt to operationalise such a continuum from classificatory to inferential types of judgement in the justificatory vocabulary of the nine discussion administrators I observed at work.

One of the aims of the coding exercise was to examine the changes that have occurred between the start of my newsroom observations in 2013 and the conclusion of my research in 2016, a comparison which is interesting given the changes in personnel and in the design of technological devices outlined in the previous two sections. Those changes led me to formulate an initial hypothesis that reasoning might have become less inferential and more classificatory in keeping with the standardisation and semi-automation inscribed in the redesign of the interface, but also with the entry of an almost completely new workforce, assuming this interrupted the informal socialisation processes that occur at workplace level. These are all the more important for the reproduction or retention of knowledge about administrating online discussion at *SME* given the absence of training and formal scripts. Indeed one might expect that scripting would form part of the response to this situation – that the lack of experiential knowledge of the new admins would oblige a more 'dogmatic' approach to applying the rules (to use a word chosen by the senior admin in 2016 to describe his own sense of what

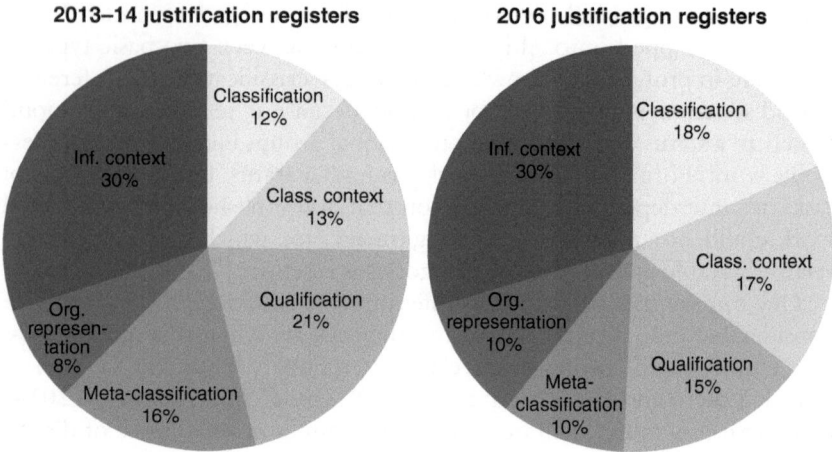

**Fig. 4.5**   Justification registers used by admins in 2013–2014 and 2016

had changed). In fact my repeat observations provide only weak support for this hypothesis: justificatory registers changed only slightly (though where they did change, it was in the expected direction), while the impact of staff turnover was more visible in increased variability between individuals than in a general shift towards rule-based justification. Figure 4.5 shows the overall distribution of justifications recorded during observation in each period, based on totals of about 150 and 75 admin decisions.

## SIX REGISTERS OF JUSTIFICATION

### *Classification (and the Production of Decisions)*

Although discretion is never absent, we can nevertheless say that it is marginal (and perhaps actively suppressed) in classificatory justification: these were judgements in which the admin used a key term from the discussion codex, or a direct synonym to explain why a comment was either deleted or allowed. A verdict is literally produced by the judgement because the choice of a word from the codex implies an unambiguous action. These were often the rapidest judgements, and could be made without reading to the end of the comment: as soon as one of the classificatory criteria for comment deletion had been fulfilled the judgement was uttered and enacted. Occasionally a word from the codex was used to justify *not* deleting a comment, an admin stating something like 'nothing vulgar' or 'doesn't insult anyone'. In these cases they were usually contesting the alerter's classification, but sometimes the category referred to was not the one the alerter had selected and the admin seemed to be vocalising an internal dispute in which a possible infringement occurred to them but was quickly rejected. This shows that even classificatory work can be a complicated cognitive process.

### Classificatory Contextualisation (and the Production of Rules)

In classificatory contextualisation admins' justifications are still part of a process of matching a case to pre-established categories (going from the abstract to the particular or the common to the specific). The difference is that they classified the case by contextualisation, not by reference to the codex. For example, they registered the type of article a discussion is attached to, and applied that knowledge to generate a rule or specify an exception or qualifier to a general rule. Notably, we find here justifications that referred to whether a comment was on- or off-topic, whether it 'reacts to the article' or 'has nothing in common with the theme'. This is a limited, standardised, form of discretionary reasoning, still rule-based (the action always followed automatically – a comment that was classified as off-topic was always deleted) but at the same time rulemaking because the classifications are not taken from the codex. Some such justifications were akin to verbal memos about how to interpret or apply a rule in a deviant case. One common 'script', for example, tells admins it is appropriate to apply different degrees of protection to different categories of discussion participant (discussant, blogger, journalist) or addressee (private person, public person, minority social group, majority social group). In the mid-2000s this was described as an unwritten rule by a former web-editor admin (2004–2008), but subsequently – in a rare example of codification – it was systematised in a guidance note written by *SME*'s UGC project manager and made available to admins as a shared Google document. Although this document had been forgotten by the time of my observations, it was apparent that admins were 'making' an equivalent kind of derivative contextual rule in justifications like the following: 'Coarse – but it's about politics – I'll let it go'; 'It wasn't pretty but it's [aimed] at a political party – they have to put up with that'; 'there's a hint of an attack on a vulnerable population group there'; 'I think he's referring to refugees – that's already broken the codex'. Classificatory contextualisation opens a slightly larger gap between judgement and action, and takes the admin through a more extended investigative process, but the inferential content is low and (as the guidance note example shows) standardisation is possible.

### Qualification (and the Production of Evidence)

Roughly at the centre of the continuum we find the two types of reasoning I have called qualification and meta-classification. The former is a type of expert evaluation, marked by references to the quality of a contribution as a knowledge artefact. To explain what I mean it is helpful to refer to the legal domain, which I have elsewhere suggested is a useful comparator for many aspects of admin work (Smith 2015). Qualifying reasoning is an important part of any legal process, where it logically precedes the application of rules: a magistrate first qualifies the facts of the dossier as a necessary prelude to deciding which paragraph of the law to apply (Weller 2007). Here we have a similar situation: most of these judgements were uttered during the thinking process, before a case was 'closed'. The verdict does not follow automatically from the utterance, because we are still at the preliminary stage of producing not decisions or rules but evidence. It was as if admins were summoning another part of themselves in the capacity of expert witnesses. Moreover it was quite often a requalifying process, initiating and justifying a sequence of cognitive steps in which the classification contained in the alert could be overridden; creating space for the possibility of a different assessment from that of the complainant. As we saw before, classificatory reasoning could also contest an alerter's judgement, but the difference lies in the next step, which is not a simple denial/refusal but a new or further investigation. These cases thus present a paradox, because the introduction of the simple classification system by which alerters are asked to choose one of four types of offence was supposed to relieve admins of 'lots of superfluous text' (the free-form justifications that alerters had hitherto supplied). But in many cases we find admins, in their sensemaking processes, needing to go back a step and reformat or reconstruct the evidence, either by making a qualitative assessment of the level or type of argument perceived (e.g. 'ironic', 'opinionated', 'daft', 'cultivated'); or to place comments on imaginary scales of quality that run, for example, from 'normal' to 'abnormal', 'valuable' to 'worthless', 'constructive' to 'unconstructive', 'sane' to 'insane', 'problematic' to 'unproblematic' or from containing an 'argument' to having 'no argument'. Such polarised continua may represent more intuitive ways of seizing the measure of things than the quasi-legal typology that the classificatory register rests on, as Boltanski et al. (1984: 5) discovered in their study of judgements in Le Monde's readers' letters department in the 1980s: journalists tasked with judging the publishability of a letter applied (often unconsciously) a 'normality' test to its stylistic qualities and its author's 'way with words' before they judged the interest of the information within it.[11]

### Metaclassification (and the Production of Order)

Metaclassification is a type of reasoning in which the admin's justification refers to an idea of rules or norms without actually 'quoting' one. Often they seemed to be interpreting the spirit rather than the letter of the law, in cases where diagnosis and treatment are not indexed one-to-one. So professional discretion to vary the rules is present in these examples, but justified at a more abstract, universal level by a framework of rules. References to what is 'standard', 'in order', 'fine' or alternatively 'out of order', 'over the edge', or 'borderline' typified this type of reasoning, where what is being produced is a sense of order. Sometimes this comes through indirectly via the production of personal rules that are not enshrined in the codex, such as 'I usually delete comments in capitals' or 'I usually delete comments containing links'. I also regarded as metaclassificatory justifications such as 'it's possible to say that in a different way' and 'it's possible to criticise politicians without name-calling' because the 'polyphonic authority' (Colin and Ducrot 2009) they invoke through the use of the passive voice reproduces a sense of order grounded in common sense or generally accepted standards.

### Organisational Representation (and the Reproduction of Values)

Finally, at the most discretionary end of the continuum are two categories of reasoning that are experience-based rather than rule-based. Justifications were coded 'organisational representation' when it was apparent that the admin was considering organisational interests in their decision-making. Often marked by use of first person plural they specify an embodied sense of what belongs and does not 'belong' in the discussion, or what 'we want' (or do not want) there. They are close to public relations work but they are less about creating or upholding the organisation's public image[12] than about reproducing the admin's sense of the values they are called upon to defend in the discussion as a representative of the organisation. Sometimes this was very direct, as in 'we've got a very broad interpretation of freedom of speech' or 'I don't want to confirm his prejudices about us', sometimes more implicit as in 'That shouldn't be there', and sometimes there was a tension with personal identifications as in: 'I was talking about this kind of thing with a colleague at lunch – how we can sometimes agree with a comment and yet have to delete it'.[13] Admins were projecting themselves into the role of representing the interests, policies, brand values, ethics or tastes of the newspaper and using this projected identity as a sort of heuristic short-cut in their decision-making. Often it was a 'how-do-I-feel?' heuristic (Delli Carpini 1999) such as 'that matches our taste' or simply 'I don't like that'. I suggest that admins felt confident enough to act on affective judgements because of their experience as members of an organisation, combined with the relatively minor consequences of getting it wrong (which is also partly an organisational value).

### Inferential Contextualisation (and the Production of Room for Manoeuvre)

> Professional thinking resembles chess. The opening diagnosis is often clear, even formulaic. So also is the endgame of treatment. The middle game [professional inference], however, relates professional knowledge, client characteristics, and chance in ways that are often obscure. (Abbott 1988: 48)

Inferential contextualisation refers to a type of discretion rooted not in an organisational identity but in a practical sense for the characteristics of the discussion as a distinct milieu, community or culture: to the types of reasoning that follow direct contact with 'human complexity' and the consequent need to treat an 'impure' problem from the point of view of a professional knowledge system (Abbott 1981). They are the cases whose solution demands a double move: closer contact with the milieu followed by abstraction, which is often inductive. I came across two situations that illustrate this type particularly well. One often occurred when an admin received an alert about a comment under a blog. As noted earlier, although *SME*'s blog system has its own volunteer admins, all alerts appear in the same admin notice list, and the on-duty web-editor would normally clear the whole list rather than ignoring the blog-related ones for a blog admin to deal with later. But in both observation periods this could occasionally produce tangible disorientation, which has a simple explanation: web-editors know most of the stories on the journalistic parts of the website, but they do not have time or reason to keep abreast of new blogs being published. Knowing what the day's news is about (having either edited or hierarchised much of it) helps them form expectations of what the discussion might be like, or should be like. They have a great deal more difficulty in constructing an 'ideal discussant' for blogs about which they only have to hand the title, especially bearing in mind that most bloggers do not follow familiar journalistic conventions when choosing headlines. They also have to deal with the possibility that the alerter and the blogger may be the same person, which is often a first additional check that is performed as they begin to contextualise. As well as paying more attention to the identity of the alerter, they have an increased tendency to click on the article in the case of blogs. They very rarely read one in detail, but they often want to see it as they try to make sense of the discussion. When even this does not suffice, a more informal type of inferential reasoning surfaces: 'blogs are the most difficult – I have to use my intuition', one admin remarked in 2016, visibly unsettled, before repeating the common refrain that 'blogs are more personal'.[14]

The second situation that helps illustrate inferential contextualisation was when an admin clicks on a user ID to look at their 'history'. Extending the investigation in this fashion takes us into the realm of reputation control, subverting the latest interface redesign and straying onto the UGC project manager's remit: 'let me look at his other contributions ... [*Researcher: what are you looking for?*] Whether he's a problem case, some sort of pattern, whether he does it frequently'. Prior to the change of interface, glancing at the 'PBV' numbers (see previous section) served an analogous purpose, prompting comments like: 'long-term discussant – worth sending him an explanation'. At stake could be the reputation of either of the users involved – the author of the targeted comment or the alerter: 'a common case – someone writing an alert just to let off steam. I often look at who sent the alert'. When making closer scrutiny of an alert an admin is effectively asking him- or herself about its status as evidence: should one regard it, for instance, as a witness statement or as an intervention in a dispute? We can perhaps even generalise this point by saying that in inferential contextualisation both alerts and comments became *events* and reasoning becomes *abductive*. An 'inferring' admin would try to work out what could have 'provoked' an alert by looking at the preceding comments. Similarly it became relevant to look at the effects comments produced: 'I don't have a problem leaving that, but first I want to see if the thread takes off and if it's a flame'.

Admins' words often placed a new case in a mental library of occurrences (recognising a 'common case', for instance). But unlike the 'memos' admins verbalised when doing classificatory contextualisation, these remarks were not, I suggest, about rulemaking but about the negotiation of room for manoeuvre and with it the self-authorisation to take a little more time to deliberate. The question of time, indeed, was central when I coded these justifications: as much as the actual choice of words, I recognised inferential reasoning by the length of time an admin thought about a decision – by the presence of an obvious 'deliberative pause' (Latour 2002) in their reasoning. But the hitch is that they did not actually stop and think – they continued clicking (or highlighting with the cursor), which leads me to believe that navigating around a comment's intertextual and hypertextual references, or clicking on a user's history, serves in part to buy time for thinking. Without prolonging the logical chain too far, in inferential contextualisation admins made room for a more extended 'middle game', simulating activity long enough to feel they have properly weighed things up.

Figure 4.5 indicates that almost half of admin decisions are arrived at via one of the two most inferential types of reasoning,[15] and the proportion is unchanged from 2013 to 2016: surprisingly, perhaps, the intervening organisational and technological changes have not either compromised the capacity or reduced the discretionary space of admins to infer. Further down the scale, we see a slight change, however, towards a more classificatory overall profile of decision-making. Classification and classificatory contextualisation account for 10% more justifications in 2016 than in 2013, with a corresponding decline in meta-classification and qualification: the personal rules of thumb or ingrained sense for what is 'standard' and the placing of arguments on scales. This matches the senior administrator's assessment (in interview) that, following the staff turnover, decision-making had become more 'dogmatic'. But these aggregate figures conceal an increased variability between individuals: whereas in 2013 the balance between more classificatory and more inferential decisions was fairly consistent between individuals, in 2016 I found two predominantly classificatory and two predominantly inferential reasoners. This would fit the hypothesis of a breakdown of informal workplace socialisation due to staff turnover. Of the three new admins, two rely mainly on classifying and qualifying, while one of the inferential reasoners is the senior admin, the only one who has worked in *SME* for a considerable time period. But one new member of staff (coming to *SME* straight from journalism school, with no previous experience of discussion administration) also frequently draws on inferential contextualisation and almost systematically clicks through to see the context of a message: further investigation is routinised as a way of testing his own typifications. He can afford to do so as long as the pace of work permits because of the lack of supervision and standardisation in the performance of discussion administration. He was unusual among all the admins observed in staunchly defending the intraprofessional status of the web-editor role, and in refusing to see it as a transitional stage in a journalist's career.

What we see, in short, is some admins going with the flow of technologically inscribed routinisation of the task, but others resisting, finding workarounds and uncovering hidden technological affordances to open a greater discretionary space and make time for longer deliberative pauses that are necessary for them to make good decisions in keeping with the maintenance of a professional identity. The stability across time of inferential reasoning could be taken as a sign that internalised rules about when to resort to inference are relatively stable and independent of technological and personnel factors, which would in itself be a sign of professionalism (Abbott 1988: 51). The increased variance between individuals, however, invites the opposite conclusion. Any interpretation, of course, has to be cautious given the extremely small number of individuals available for observation in a single case study.

## Coping with Professional Status Strain on the Front-Line

Admin work can be conceived of as front-line professional work, because the admin is right there intervening in that 'user-generated' space that co-exists with and reacts to the fruits of professional knowledge work. There are many cases of front-line professional work in which 'human complexity' is so insistent that inference becomes an everyday necessity (Abbott 1981). So, for example, in an ethnographic study of farm inspectors whose job it was to control farmers' compliance with the conditions attached to EU farm subsidies, Weller showed how their work bore little resemblance to 'the conception promoted by administrative science: an agent as a simple executor, a neutral operator mechanically applying the law' (2007: 724). The comparison is particularly pertinent because his subjects were also low-status front-line professionals, often employed seasonally and given only basic training. In a later paper, he highlighted the paradox this creates for the sociology of professions:

> Is it correct to draw from the tensions these *contrôleurs* experience, and the strategies they deploy to adjust [to] specific situations, a deep and strong discretionary capacity? Yes, if one follows Lipsky, considering with him that they act as 'professionals'. Yes, if one estimates that they intervene as an autonomous and coherent group. Yes, if one focuses on 'the actor', defining the totality through which work, representations and experiments are reported. But there is a problem here! The public controllers we followed during their visits to farms do not generally have the independence authentic professionals have. They are typically not official civil servants, but rather merely temporary employees engaged for few months. (Weller 2012: 5)

The question Weller asks – should we see the liberal employment of inferential reasoning in knowledge work as a sign of professionalism? – poses similar difficulties in the case of discussion administrators. I suggest that an adequate answer has to recognise that there are two competing, but not necessarily incompatible explanations for the large dose of inference in this type of work:

- it's about restoring or retaining a link with the (user/client/local) milieu, with getting a better feel for the community and its ways;[16]
- it's about restoring a 'dignified' professionalism to a degraded professional routine by elevating it above the mechanical application of rules.

The former is relevant to a struggle for external legitimacy (in the public arena), the latter to a struggle for internal legitimacy (both at the workplace level and at the level of intrapersonal identity work).

What I think we're looking at is a transversal knowledge practice whose agents are juggling amateurising and professionalising dynamics as they master the art of discussion administration and striving to balance a dual accountability to internal and external publics or internal and external criteria for judging quality. Admins were doing something similar to the administrators in Swinglehurst and Greenhalgh's (2015) study of how medical patient records are produced and coded in doctors' surgeries, who tended to add more and more information to records until doctors complained that 'it doesn't fit on the screen'. The interpretation of the authors was that the doctors were practical reasoners, conscious of their need to make rapid decisions in pressurised situations, while the administrators were acting as patient advocates. One of the reasons why admins often want more information than the streamlined view provided by the interface could also be that they instinctively adopt the role of 'reader's advocate'. This was most explicit in the case of discussion below blogs, where admins often sensed it was appropriate to adjust their criteria to get inside the head of the blogger or understand the expectations of a highly localised discussion community. But when they extend or expand the investigation and go looking for more information they also do so, I contend, in order to satisfy their professional pride and the need for day-to-day on-the-job satisfaction. This was apparent when they inserted 'deliberative pauses'. In theory, the primary function of professional inference is to guard against errors, and from a strictly utilitarian point of view admins probably do more inference than is necessary, since admin decisions are less consequential and more reversible than most professional judgements.[17] Inference thus allows admins to do two very different things: distance themselves from journalistic standards in order to approximate the quality criteria that matter to specific groups of discussants, and restore a certain methodological professionalism (the privilege to open a discretionary space) to an otherwise degraded newsroom task.

What does all this mean for journalism and for media organisations? Abbott's notion of professional purity is useful in tracing some of the implications because of its connection with the question of social jurisdictions. Defined as the ability to exclude non-professional or irrelevant professional issues from practice, Abbott suggests that professional purity is the underlying variable determining intraprofessional (as opposed to extraprofessional) status, such that 'the lowest status professionals are those who deal with problems from which the human complexities are not or cannot be removed' (1981: 824). That explains why one finds inference at both ends of intraprofessional status hierarchies – in a profession's most abstract, specialised regions as well as on the front line: 'the great exception to the routine theory – the low status of non-routine front line professional work – is explained by the extreme professional impurity of that work' (ibid.: 825). It is also the 'human complexities' of online discussion, and the 'impurity' of its issues, that explain the persistently high prevalence of inferential contextualisation in admins' judgements, if inference can be seen as a means, available to the knowledgeable individual, by which 'messy' client issues can be translated into professionally respectable problems and made compatible with the professional knowledge system (ibid.: 826).

But (to echo Weller) there is a problem here! The symbolic compensation for most groups of front-line professionals is high public esteem, and the admin certainly does not enjoy the charismatic extraprofessional status that, in other contexts, attaches to those who confront and control disorder (sickness, insanity, criminality, etc.) in direct contact with the public (Abbott 1981: 829). It would be difficult to claim that newsroom careers that start with admin work are an example of the way professions cope with tendencies towards excessive purification – and the long-term danger it poses to public jurisdictions – by obliging at least the novices to 'get their hands dirty', notably because the impersonal form of administration that has evolved excludes the possibility of journalism or media organisations extracting much extraprofessional credit from admins' interactions with the public. This is a missed opportunity for journalism, as the very existence of such a contact-heavy task is an invitation for jurisdictional work in the public arena. Yet there is no tangible evidence that either journalism or organisations have been able to use this new point of contact with the public to renew public legitimacy.

## NOTES

1. Here I prefer the term administration, largely because it is the term used in *SME* and most other Slovak newspapers, but also because I understand moderation as active facilitation – attempting to steer or stimulate discussion – which is not what happens in the vast majority of news portals, including *SME.*
2. It includes only those people who actually made decisions about comments in a given year, not all those who had administrator rights. It also excludes specialised admins, who intervened only in non-news sections of the *SME* website, notably the blog admins, as distinct from the blogger admins (see later).
3. VIP bloggers are accorded greater visibility on the main blog page (and also by the very fact that they can be viewed as a separate list) and are allowed to administrate the discussion beneath their own articles.
4. It seems unlikely that this in itself caused senior journalists to intervene more often, in a wish to 'keep an eye' on the online division. Web-editors were assigned to a particular newsdesk and sat among their home, foreign or economics news colleagues even though they belonged formally to the

online division. According to all witnesses I talked to, *SME* never suffered from the sharp cultural-organisational cleavages between print and online that were reported to exist at many other newspapers in the early 2000s.

5. Quotations are from these interviews. Respondents are identified by their role combination and the period in which they administered discussion (usually but not always their full term of employment at *SME*).

6. There is also arguably a resemblance of a different sort between the two types of work: as will be explained, admin work involves *reacting to alerts*, which is a metaphor Estienne has used to describe the work of web-editors as they respond to the flux of incoming newswires and press releases which they have to monitor and process (2007: 179).

7. Asked what qualities made for a good administrator, the deputy editor-in-chief said that they should not enjoy reading the discussions, because enjoyment tends to provoke involvement, which he firmly believed was out of keeping with dispassionate judgment and effective arbitration.

8. The Guardian, among others, developed a system in which 'risky' users can be put on probation so that their comments are pre-moderated until they convince admins they can 'contribute reasonably' (Reich 2011: 110).

9. The post changed hands in January 2015.

10. Abbott illustrates this point with the following historical example: 'Freudian psychiatry succeeded because the routine aspect of the system made it comprehensible to laymen, while the nonroutine aspect justified the formation of a specialized core to apply it'. By contrast, Adolf Meyer's rival system, which referred nearly all cases to formal inference by trained therapists, 'seemed like a mass of personal judgements', and hence failed to gain the same public legitimacy even though, therapeutically, it was just as successful (Abbott 1988: 52).

11. Boltanski et al found that journalists were often drawn towards grammatical features of letters in judging normality, which was also the case in admin work. Inevitably, the research situation, simply by slowing down the task, occasionally disrupted these intuitive judgements, and on one occasion prompted an administrator to question the reliability of one of his own instinctive normality tests: 'Interesting case – normally I delete those sorts of comments straight away, but now that I've taken more time to read it I'm going to pass it. Often it's just a matter of poor grammatical habits'.

12. The results of admin decisions are only reviewable by two other individuals – the alerter and the accused, and the latter only if the comment is deleted. The rest of the public can see that a comment has been deleted (it is replaced by a standard phrase) but can no longer read it.

13. Moral dilemmas resulting from a disjuncture between the rules people are asked to enforce and the convictions they hold about those rules have been found in other types of frontline professional work (e.g. Weller 2012: 5).

14. I sensed that he was not claiming intuition as a professional competence but rather admitting that he felt he was having to stray beyond his professional competence, even if one could infer a professional conscientiousness when someone takes care not to presume what kind of comments fit with the discursive identity of an unfamiliar blog.

15. The darker the shading the more inferential the reasoning. In fact, the spectrum of reasoning we are looking at is certainly extendable to more inferential types of reasoning which admins exclude from consideration given the relatively low costs of errors and the low priority accorded to discussion administration.

16. In the context of the history of admining at *SME* this can be interpreted as a restoration of the ethos of the blogger admins.

17. A bit like the provisional diagnoses made in hospital triage, a 'bad' classificatory decision in principle gets a second chance: a new alert can be sent about the same comment that was 'erroneously' passed, while the author of an 'erroneously' deleted comment can complain by email, or in the discussion.

## References

Abbott, A. (1981). Status and status strain in the professions. *American Journal of Sociology, 86*(4), 819–835.

Abbott, A. (1988). *The system of professions. An essay on the division of expert labor.* Chicago & London: University of Chicago Press.

Boltanski, L., Darré, Y., & Schiltz, M.-A. (1984). La dénonciation. *Actes de la recherche en sciences sociales, 51,* 3–40.

Chateauraynaud, F. (2003). *Prospéro. Une technologie littéraire pour les sciences humaines.* Paris: CNRS ÉDITIONS.

Colin, M., & Ducrot, O. (2009). Mise au point sur la polyphonie. *Langue française, 164,* 33–43.

Degand, A. (2012). *Le journalisme face au web: La reconfiguration des pratiques et des répresentations professionelles dans les rédactions belges francophones.* Louvain-la-Neuve: Presses Universitaires de Louvain.

Delli Carpini, M. (1999). In search of the information citizen: What Americans know about politics and why it matters. *The Communication Review, 4,* 129–164.

Diakopoulos, N., & Naaman, M. (2011). Towards quality discourse in online news comments. In *Proceedings of the ACM 2011 conference on computer supported cooperative work,* Hangzhou, China.

Ericsson, K., & Simon, H. (1993). *Protocol analysis: Verbal reports as data* (revised edition). Cambridge, MA: MIT Press.

Estienne, Y. (2007). *Le journalisme après Internet*. Paris: L'Harmattan.
Ihlebaek, K., & Krumsvik, A. (2015). Editorial power and public participation in online newspapers. *Journalism, 16*(4), 470–487.
Latour, B. (2002). *La fabrique du droit. Une ethnographie du Conseil d'État*. Paris: La Découverte.
Misnikov, Y. (2010). Discursive qualities of public discussion on the Russian internet: Testing the Habermasian communicative action empirically. In F. De Cindio, A. Macintosh, & C. Peraboni (Eds.), *Online deliberation. Fourth International Conference OD2010*. Leeds: University of Leeds.
Mitchelstein, E. (2011). Catharsis and community: Divergent motivations for audience participation in online newspapers and blogs. *International Journal of Communication, 5*, 2014–2034.
Paterson, C., & Domingo, D. (Eds.). (2008). *Making online news: The ethnography of new media production*. New York: Peter Lang Publishing.
Reich, Z. (2011). User comments: The transformation of participatory space. In J. Singer et al. (Eds.), *Participatory journalism. Guarding open gates at online newspapers* (pp. 96–117). Malden, MA & Oxford: Wiley-Blackwell.
Robinson, S. (2010). Traditionalists vs. convergers. Textual privilege, boundary work, and the journalist-audience relationship in the commenting policies of online news sites. *Convergence: The International Journal of Research into New Media Technologies, 16*(1), 125–143.
Ruiz, C., Domingo, D., Micó, J., Díaz-Noci, J., Meso, K., & Masip, P. (2011). Public sphere 2.0? The democratic qualities of citizen debates in online newspapers. *The International Journal of Press/Politics, 16*(4), 463–487.
Smith, S. (2015). Mezi právnickým a žurnalistickým zdůvodňováním dovednosti administrátorů internetové diskuse ve slovenském deníku. In E. Bútorová & V. Veverková (Eds.), *Úskalia žurnalistickej a masmediálnej komunikácie v súčasnosti. Zborník z 1. ročníka medzinárodnej vedeckej konferencie Úskalia žurnalistickej a masmediálnej komunikácie v súčasnosti (Nitra 22. 10. 2014)*, Nitra: Univerzita Konštantína Filozofa, pp. 89–106.
Sumpter, R. (2000). Daily newspaper editors' audience construction routines: A case study. *Critical Studies in Media Communication, 17*(3), 334–346.
Swinglehurst, D., & Greenhalgh, T. (2015). Caring for the patient, caring for the record: An ethnographic study of 'back office' work in upholding quality of care in general practice. *BMC Health Services Research, 15*, 177.
Wallander, L., & Molander, A. (2014). Disentangling professional discretion: A conceptual and methodological approach. *Professions & Professionalism, 4* (3). Available at https://journals.hioa.no/index.php/pp/article/view/808 [accessed 10.7.16].
Weller, J.-M. (2007). La disparition des bœufs du Père Verdon, Travail administratif ordinaire et statut de la qualification. *Droit et société, 67*, 713–755.

Weller, J.-M. (2011). Comment décrire ce qu'on ne voit pas? Le devoir d'hésitation des juges de proximité au travail. *Sociologie du Travail*, 53(3), 349–368.

Weller, J.-M. (2012) *An ethnographer among street-level bureaucrats and new public management*. Solvay Brussels School of Economics and Management, DULBEA and Centre Emile Bernheim, Université Libre de Bruxelles Working Paper WP-CEB. Available at: https://hal-enpc.archives-ouvertes.fr/hal-00837637 [accessed 10.7.16].

# CHAPTER 5

# The Conversations Between Participatory Journalists and Critical Publics

**Abstract** Examining a corpus of discussion exchanges between journalists and members of the public at a newspaper committed to participatory journalism, Smith tests the performativity of different types of comment in eliciting responses from journalists, highlighting the success of accusations and metajournalistic comments (talk about journalism). Interviews with participating journalists confirm the practical difficulties of integrating discussion into existing newsroom routines and the importance of technological constraints. When journalists engage they display two strategies that correspond to Abbott's model of professional legitimisation – process and authority arguments – but occasionally they use a new strategy. For although even in the discussion most reporters equate professionalism with neutrality and distance, a few adopt a polemical discursive identity as they learn to talk credibly in poorly scripted situations.

**Keywords** Accusation · Discursive identity · Metajournalistic · Polemic · Public legitimacy

This chapter foregrounds the third of this book's organising concepts – competences. It shows how online discussion can become a space for practising, performing and displaying journalistic skills (but not necessarily the same skills that 'normal' journalistic writing requires) and for criticising and defending competences (in the double sense of skills and jurisdictions).

© The Author(s) 2017
S. Smith, *Discussing the News*, Palgrave Studies in Science,
Knowledge and Policy, DOI 10.1007/978-3-319-52965-3_5

Examining how competences are tested in metajournalistic discussion exchanges can be used as a point of entry to the debate about how the profession is responding to the participatory turn, viewed as a jurisdictional challenge (Abbott 1988). The source of this participatory imperative is highly diffuse and exerts a differential influence on individual practice: as will be shown, even in an organisation committed to participatory journalism, the onus to discuss is not internalised as a strong *organisational* rule but more as a new example of *professional* good practice, an obligation concomitant with the gradual renegotiation of the contract of communication that governs a journalist's discursive identity in relation to a public, itself increasingly critical of journalism as an institution. As such it is accepted or contested according to journalists' differing dispositions and field positions.

As it has become a cliché for journalists to say – and perhaps to advise novices – 'don't read the comments!', exceptions to this commonsense wisdom are particularly useful to study: how do we account for the fact that some journalists not only read comments but also respond to them? When I asked 12 journalists at *Denník N* to try and verbalise the rules-of-thumb they apply when considering whether to enter the discussion, they tended either to draw on spatial metaphors or to typify arguments, referring both to the types of arguments they want to react to and the types they want to perform (or avoid performing). For illustration, Table 5.1 shows how different – sometimes diametrically opposed – these personal rules-of-thumb can be.

**Table 5.1** Journalistic rules-of-thumb for discussion participation (paraphrased from interviews)

| | |
|---|---|
| Spatial metaphors | I don't discuss because I've got a platform elsewhere |
| | It suits me to be the journalist hidden behind the story |
| | Letting the public know we're not from another planet |
| | Countering the public image that journalists think they inhabit 'Olympus' |
| Typifying discussants' argumentation | Don't respond to opinions |
| | Don't react to praise |
| | You have to correct disinformation/conspiracy theories |
| | You have to react to a meaningful counter-argument |
| Minding one's own argumentation | I avoid polemicising |
| | I try and start polemics |
| | Not exactly to conceal one's opinion, but not to display it |
| | As a non-mainstream paper we can allow ourselves to go further |

The paradigm shift from a *journalism on information* to a *journalism of communication* (Brin, Charron and De Bonville 2004) provides a partial explanatory framework for the reconceptualisation that is (or may be) underway – for the valorisation of 'conversational' competences, for example – but it fails to capture all of what is happening, and I suggest that an alternative framing is also useful: the resurgence of some of the norms and roles associated with an older *journalism of opinion*, valorising less a conversational than an argumentative competence on the part of journalists. This can be seen as a way of coming to terms with the dillution or dispersion of journalism's power to set the agenda for public debate in the new informational environment.

## The Routines for Organising and Engaging in Discussion

The data for this chapter come from the second case study site, *Denník N*. They consist of a corpus of discussion threads from the first six months of operation of the newspaper, supplemented by interviews with journalists in which I used examples from their own portfolios to discuss their criteria for engaging in discussion, their feelings about it and their sense of how discussion relates to 'core' journalistic roles and discursive identities. The interviews played a vital part in data interpretation at an intermediate analytical stage. Twelve were carried out, selecting two representatives of each of the main departments (domestic news, foreign news, economics, comment and opinion), two representatives of specialist sections (culture and science) and two external correspondents notable for their enthusiasm for participatory journalism, but also interesting because they do not work from the newsroom, which might be expected to influence their working routines and discursive identities, on the assumption that they are less strongly socialised by an organisational or workplace habitus.

The key distinguishing feature of managing discusion at $N$ is that two pivotal decisions – whether to open discussion and when and how to engage in discussion – are devolved to the authors of most articles. This policy, though, was implemented 'softly' by management, aware of likely resistance to any obligation to 'do' discussion:

> Those are the rules: the author is responsible for the quality of the discussion, but we've never forced anyone to go into the discussion. They don't get penalised [if they don't]! We were just glad that some journalists began

to think of discussion as something that doesn't come from another planet. (Deputy editor-in-chief for online journalism)

After a very 'participative' start, the percentage of discussions open (below articles by in-house staff) fell from 70% in January 2015 to around 30% in June 2015, and the monthly total of comments by journalists from 80 in January to around 20 by mid-year. These kinds of statistics are not collected at $N$ and the previous figures are based on my own calculations. When shown to the deputy editor-in-chief for online journalism, they appeared to cause him some concern, and he asked for permission to circulate my graphs to members of the newsroom. They were accompanied by the following email:

> Let me remind you of the agreement:
>
> – We automatically open discussion below comment pieces and interviews
> – It's good if the author discusses. It verifiably improves the quality of debate
> – Authors can open discussion beneath other kinds of text at their own initiative. The stats show that some, like colleague X are already doing so.[1]

In fact, resistance stemming from professional experience or instinct was probably less important in explaining the initial decline than technological factors. The steepest drop in discussions open occurred between February and March 2015, which coincided with a change in one of the default settings in the content management system. Before then an author or editor publishing an article needed to untick a box in order to disable discussion. But this created a problem:

> We still weren't used to that system – to that on/off column. In the system the button's a bit, well, hidden. At the beginning it often got forgotten and so the debate stayed switched on. (Reporter and print editor, foreign news section)

The default setting was therefore altered so that the box was initially blank and an author needed to tick it if they wanted to activate discussion. The logic for the change of setting was flawless – one needs to legislate for the inevitability of forgetfulness, and it's better if discussion is accidentally off than accidentally on:

It happens that you don't reflect on it. We reckoned that those situations would happen very often and asked ourselves: what's better as the default? Is the damage greater if discussion's on when it should be off or if it's off when it should be on? And given the time pressures people work under, we decided it's best if it's off. (Deputy editor-in-chief for online journalism)

But the extent of its impact was much greater than anticipated. This sequence from an interview with the editor of the comment & opinion section[2] encapsulates the situation afterwards:

Who decides about it? Sometimes I decide, when I put an article on the web and I click that box to allow discussion. But sometimes I just forget and I don't click it [laughing]
  *Researcher: And what happens then?*
Either it stays like that, or someone else notices and opens it. I normally put all the 'argument' section on the web, and some of the comment pieces when I'm on duty, and I should always open discussion, but if I forget then it's simply . . . the human factor! [laughing]
  *Researcher: Because of the pace of work?*
No, there's a routine set of tasks – headline, sub-headline, paste in the text, make adjustments, insert subtitles, insert the author's name and then, right at the very bottom, there it is. But sometimes I go back up [the screen] to add a photo, categorise the article, and then I simply forget. It's irrational, but that's just how it works. (Print editor, comment & opinion section)

Apart from forgetfulness, some journalists from other sections admitted that the change in the system gave them an excuse to leave the discussion switched off more often than they would if the default had been 'on'.

Moderating and contributing to discussion, if there are a lot of reactions, takes a hell of a lot of time. So now – it's not that I decided not to engage on principle, I just want to concentrate on the things that, you know, one ought to be doing – writing articles. And after that system change it was less of a conundrum, because given that I knew how little time I have, it made little sense. (Reporter, foreign news section)

This remark – from one of the most prolific discussion participants among the staff at *N* – shows the importance that simple changes in technical configuration can have on the ways peripheral tasks are integrated into work routines. The way the system was now set up gave him the licence to take a decision (limiting his engagement in discussion) that he could justify in terms of professional and organisational priorities but which, he hints, had been psychologically more difficult to do when he needed to take an active step – unclicking the box in the content management system – to disable discussion. Now that he could do it just by 'forgetting' it seemed easier. Later in the interview he said he would prefer it if decisions about permitting discussion were made more collectively, and if the web-editors made themselves more available to advise authors about an article's suitability for discussion based on both content and moderation time considerations.[3]

If the routine for opening discussion is so heavily affected by its technological 'equipment', we ought to be attentive to similar factors that could affect the engagement routine. Above all we need to treat it *as a routine*, whose performance depends on how well it is integrated into the daily sequences of tasks journalists carry out. A minority of interviewees said discussion-related tasks were quite compatible with their routines:

> You only need glance at it once an hour, it's not really moderation in the proper sense.
> *Researcher: And what about at home in the evening?*
> Yes [I look at it], it's not a big burden, it's minimal. (Reporter, economics section)

A colleague spoke of particularly enjoying engaging in discussion at weekends – 'although even then it depends on what's happening at work' (Reporter, economics section).

Regardless of how much or little they actually discuss most interviewees said that their propensity to do so depended on the availability of time and the kind of day they were having. They also concurred about the importance of monitoring the discussion for the first few hours after publication or its appearance on the journal's home page and Facebook profile, and reacting quickly to keep the discussion 'alive'. These two sets of temporal conditions – the rhythm of the working day and the rhythm of of the discussion – could be in or out of synch, but the clear priority given to former precluded being able to choose the ideal time to perform discussion-related tasks, which generally meant that discussion was dealt with only in leftover slots of the working day – in down-time:

> There's a big dose of laziness in it. I can see that I'm maybe capable of doing the discussion up until lunch, when the day's less busy – that's also when I

deal with emails. After lunch, when I have phone calls to make and an article to write I never go back to the discussion. (Reporter, domestic news section)

In this case, however, my interviewee found a fortuitous logic in his task temporality:

If we're talking about texts that were published late evening, then the moment when I'll monitor the discussion will be those first few posts, the first six hours, let's say [of the following day]. I certainly won't return to it the next evening or in two days' time.[4]

Not all reporters, however, have such a structured working day, and then a clash of routines – the journalist's and the discussants' – could arise:

With me it's very haphazard. If I'm out at a press conference or on a report from morning and my text came out the previous evening, then I just don't have the possibility to follow the discussion that morning, I don't have that time-slot, I'm not at the computer. Or else it comes out in the evening, it gets onto Facebook at six in the morning but I don't get up until 8, and people start discussing as soon as it's on Facebook.[5] (Reporter, economics section)

Other factors that aggravated the problem of timing during the period of my observations at N stemmed from the 'primitive' technical design of the discussion system, a frequent object of complaint among journalists. In particular it lacked an email notification facility (to notify a commenter that someone had replied to their contribution) or a visual means of distinguishing new comments since a user's last login, which complicated the task of administration. Some journalists felt these factors negatively affected their willingness to engage in discussion:

Just now I was talking to [the social media editor] and I said it would be great if I got notifications when someone reacted to me, so that I didn't have to proactively control it. For instance if a discussion takes off under one of my older articles it's uncontrollable because I don't have time to monitor them. (Reporter, economics section)

What annoys me is that you can't set up notifications, for when someone reacts to you. It's completely primitive at N. If there are 100 comments then, sorry. Sometimes I only notice one [that I want to respond to] three weeks later. (External contributor)

> I certainly don't have time to look at a two weeks-old interview in case something new has appeared...You know we still don't have a properly programmed system – if something new appears, I have to refresh the page and scroll through it all. We're still waiting for something like we had at *SME*, where new contributions showed up in colour. (External reporter)

Estimates of how long one ought to follow the discussion ranged from about 6 to 10 hours, derived from the half-life of two key artefacts for the generation of discussion activity: the length of time a typical article remains on the home page of the journal and the turnover rate of Facebook timelines. The 'first few hours' rule was also connected to an instrumental or preventive conception of the journalist's role in discussion:

> You've got to nip it in the bud, when something's still developing. (Reporter, culture section)
> To catch the first reactions. (Deputy editor-in-chief and commentator)

This sense of urgency (a sense, perhaps, that the pace of online discussion is even faster than that of online journalism) could legitimise conventions that differ from normal journalistic writing. For example, citing a source in English was seen as okay in the discussion chiefly for reasons of speed, when the same source would need to be translated before publication in an article.

## The Discursive Identity of the Journalist as Discussant

In the remainder of the chapter I look at how journalists engaged with the public on the occasions when they joined in discussions at *N*. My analysis is based on 112 discussion threads from the first half of 2015. I excluded threads with more than 50 comments both for manageability (each comment had to be read and coded) but more importantly for methodological reasons: I was interested in finding out what type of comments journalists choose to respond to, and I assumed that in very long threads they were unlikely to have had time or inclination to read the whole discussion, and their selection would be determined partly by chance. Put another way, long threads are likely to contain numerous response-worthy comments that the journalist simply did not notice, and as such it would be dangerous to infer rules about what constitutes response-worthiness based on the categorisation of comments in long threads.

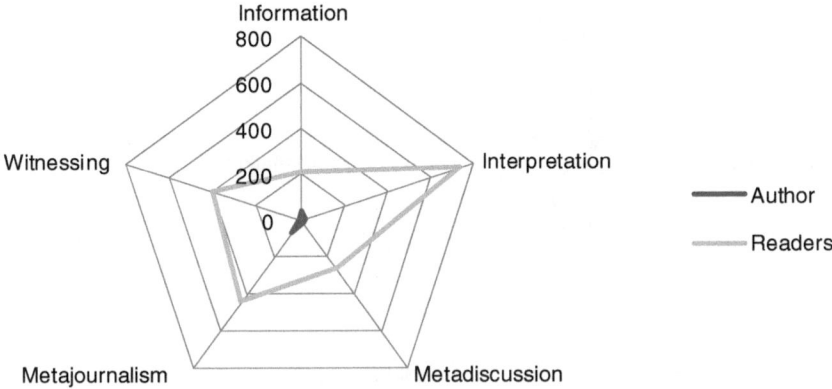

**Fig. 5.1** Comment orientation in threads where journalists participated in absolute numbers

Initially, each comment was coded for its orientation, distinguishing between five broad categories: information, interpretation, witnessing, metadiscussion and metajournalism.[6] Figure 5.1 shows the distribution of comment orientation, as well as illustrating the proportion of comments by readers and journalists (recall that these are not figures for the whole site, but only for the sub-set of threads which contained at least one journalist comment and no more than 50 comments in total).

Even at a news portal that is trying to be participative one can see that journalist comments represent a tiny fraction of total comments.[7] If we display the same data as percentages by participant type (Fig. 5.2) it's easier to compare the orientation of reader and journalist comments, and one sees clearly that readers, predictably, do much more interpreting and witnessing than journalists, who in turn provide more information. But the greatest discrepancy is in the metajournalistic category. If we add a third line showing the orientation of the comments to which journalists replied (Fig. 5.3) we see that its shape corresponds quite closely to the profile of journalist comments. This implies that there are particular comment types that journalists significantly over- and under-select, and that they usually respond 'in kind'.[8] The standout case is the metajournalistic register. In other words: comment on the journalism rather than the subject of an article, and you are considerably more likely to get a response from a journalist at $N$.[9]

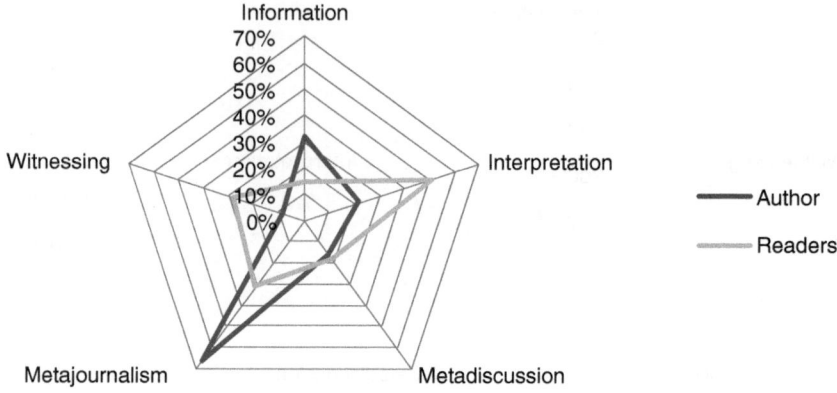

**Fig. 5.2** Comment orientation in threads where journalists participated in percentages

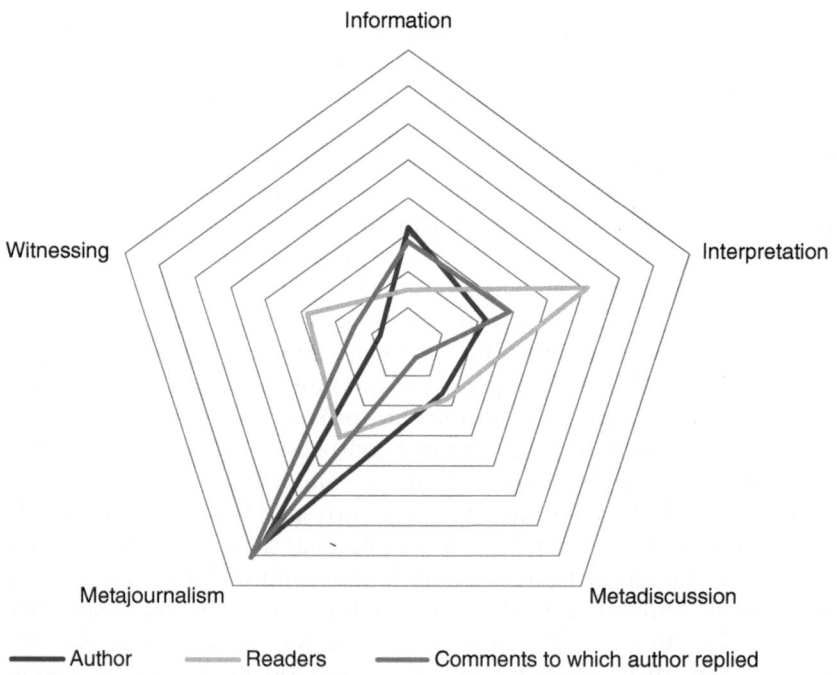

**Fig. 5.3** Comment orientation showing comments to which journalists replied

In the next stage of analysis I therefore looked more closely at the 82 metajournalistic exchanges in the corpus. Re-reading the comments that initiated exchanges it quickly became apparent that besides their metajournalistic function the overwhelming majority contain an explicit or implicit *accusation*, and so I re-coded them from this perspective, distinguishing between field-internal, field-external and specialist accusation or critique.[10] Partly informed by Abbott's sociology of professions (1988) I coded journalists' responses distinguishing between four argumentative registers: process arguments, authority arguments, polemic and acknowledgement.[11]

Combining the accusatory and response registers allows us to see whether there are typical sequences or adjacency pairs in these metajournalistic exchanges. Figure 5.4 shows that each type of accusation does indeed tend to provoke a different type of response: internal accusations are most commonly responded to with process arguments, external accusations have a certain association with authority arguments, and specialist accusations are followed most often by acknowledgements. This makes intuitive sense, and tends to confirm Abbott's observations about how professions construct and maintain public legitimacy.

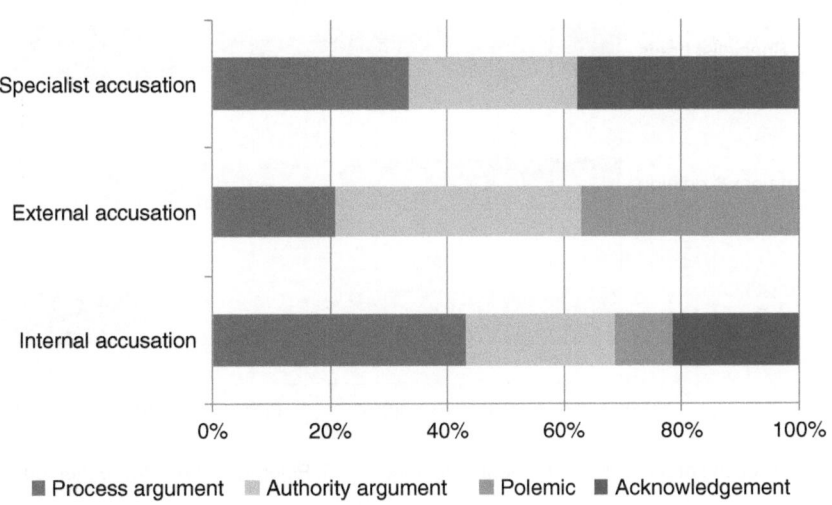

**Fig. 5.4** How do journalists respond to metajournalistic accusations?

According to Abbott, audiences address professional communities in two capacities: as recipients of services and as judges of general jurisdictional claims (Abbott 1988: 166). We could treat some metajournalistic discussion as an example of a high-status client group pre-professionalising their demands for services (evident in a lot of the field-internal accusations and the liberal use of technical jargon in some of these exchanges). The journalistic propensity to respond using process arguments might therefore be seen as a normal professional instinct to maintain the loyalty of a prized client group (ibid.: 127). But some metajournalistic critique is likely to implicate a more critical public, actively participating in the negotiation of jurisdictional claims not as a consumer of journalistic services and products but as one of the arenas in which abstract authority claims are settled (ibid.: 166). This type of claim is implicit or explicit in a lot of the field-external accusations in the corpus, and might explain the frequent recourse of journalists to arguments of authority, testifying to a need to borrow authority from other professional or expert groups.

Figure 5.5 shows the correspondence between journalists' argumentative repertoires and their rubric. General news rubrics were the most

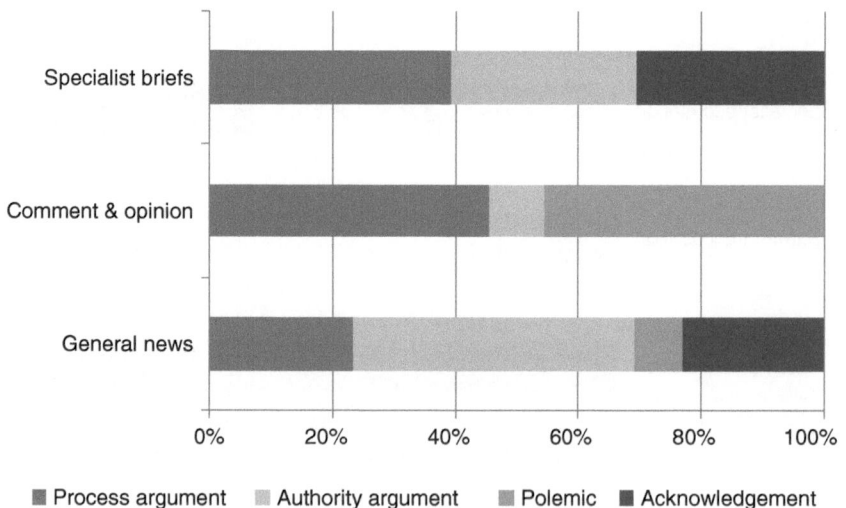

**Fig. 5.5** Journalist responses to metajournalistic accusations by rubric

diversified in their argumentative strategies – the only ones to draw on all four types. Their strongest preference was for authority arguments. One might have expected authority arguments to have been the preserve of specialist journalists, whose very discursive identity straddles two fields, but although they do use them, they occur more frequently in the discussion contributions of journalists from the general news desk. Many of these were coded as authority arguments because they contained hyperlinks to sources presented as authoritative. It might therefore be that the use of this discursive register in general rubrics is connected to the ease of linking to web sources and the option for journalists to display expertise by knowing where to look – in which case there is a certain ambiguity about whether some of the link-providing responses are actually authority or process arguments. Journalists from specialist rubrics often begin with an acknowledgement of thanks. Where they go on to make a rebuttal they draw on process arguments rather more frequently than authority arguments.[12] Journalists from specialist rubrics were the only ones never to engage in polemics, which were largely the preserve of the one commentator in the sample, whose other main mode of response was the process argument.

It's worth pausing to reflect on the particular case of discussion below comment and opinion pieces since, in common with a lot of other newspapers, the policy at *N* gives a high priority to discussion below commentary, for both commercial and democratic reasons. The polemical style of the lone – but, with 21 discussion contributions, highly prolific – discussing commentator fits naturally with an opinion-based discursive identity, a willingness to implicate oneself in one's arguments, and a treatment of discussion as a milieu in which conflict, dichotomy and denunciation are legitimate. If Charron and de Bonville are correct to see the origins of the journalistic opinion piece in a borrowing from oratory traditions (2004: 207), then commentary assumes an ostensive dimension that indicates an intention to express an opinion (and not just present the facts) in a conflictual arena modelled on public speaking and above all parliamentary debate. Once an author has assumed this particular discursive identity, it logically follows that they should assume a corresponding 'discussion identity'. It remains the case, however, that this journalist was the exception. What do we then make of the decision of all the other commentators not to engage? For many of them this is a firm point of principle, which can arguably also be derived from an opinion-based discursive identity.

Thus, in interview, a non-participating commentator explained his decision not to engage in discussion as follows:

> I don't do it, just like I don't sign petitions, because I have the opportunity to express myself elsewhere in other ways – my opinion goes straight onto the web, straight into the paper!

Aside from expressing a professional sense of craft (as if, priding himself on his rhetorical skills, he 'takes his punishment' in the event that he has failed to convince) we can also see here a claim of public influence and a concomitant exposure to criticism, accepted as the price to pay for public visibility. The diametrically opposed attitudes of different editorialists – most choosing not to engage, one choosing to engage frequently and polemically – can thus be seen as equally consistent with a strong discursive identity and a willingness to 'take' criticism according to an agonistic conception of the public sphere.

## Examples of Common Accusation-Response Sequences

In the final section I want to illustrate the principal types of metajournalistic exchange found in my corpus based on several worked examples, juxtaposing extracts from discussion below articles with journalists' interpretations or reflections as captured in my interviews.

### 1. *Internal accusation – process argument*[13]

(News flash, economics reporter)

>Miss journalist, you've an error in the first sentence, when you're controlling hospital contracts and exposing scandals, you might occasionally check your own work...

≫Hello, thank you for spotting the error, which I've now corrected... The text was published two minutes after the President's official statement arrived, so it's a relief that readers only spotted two typos.

> Interview: 'Because I have the feeling that some people really think that we've got two days for it'.

The first example illustrates very mundanely how a process argument can be deployed as a legitimising strategy. According to Abbott professionals maintain legitimacy by cultivating audiences' literacy in their specialist area, for example by sharing certain insights and terminology ('trade secrets'). On that reading, the journalist in this example is working on the assumption that 'The more understanding users have of the journalistic process, the more understanding they may have for this process' (Groenhart 2012: 197).

### 2. *External accusation – authority argument*

(Contextual article, foreign affairs reporter)
The second example is an exchange which followed a journalist's first intervention in a discussion thread. A discussant had accused him of attacking Christianity in a report contextualising the 2015 Slovak referendum about the status of gay couples (the article provided an overview of the results of similar votes in other countries). His first intervention simply refuted that accusation. A second discussant then joined the debate:
>If your contribution wasn't so sad it would be funny. Just as lobby groups order pre-election polls to massage public opinion, so your homo-lobby is softening up society with its statistics based on samples of 1000 respondents...
This opening shows the vulnerability of a journalist who engages in the discussion to external critique: the moment they start discussing they are more easily held accountable to socially available norms. In opening with a reference to the author's contribution (rather than their article), the discussant seems to authorise him/herself to adopt a more conflictual tone, even though the object of the accusation is information provided in the article, and not mentioned in the journalist's preceding comment.
≫The European Social Survey is a respected, Europe-wide survey of public opinion, going since 2002. It's one of the most widely used datasets among social scientists. If you're impugning the integrity of the ESS, we really don't have much to talk about [LINK]. Have a nice day.

> Interview: 'I took that one as a quasi political scientist [laughing]...If someone attacks me for my sources, and I know that I'm on firm ground, then I react. Otherwise you risk creating the impression among other readers that this discussant's dubious facts are fine and mine are bad. In my opinion you've got to react to that'.

In this case the journalist's strategy rests on an authority argument. It is an example of how professionals also maintain legitimacy by borrowing authority from other spheres and referring to knowledge and actors expected to have greater credibility in a given context (in this case social science). When providing hyperlinks twin sources of authority are invoked: the authority of the source linked, but also the authority of a culture of blogging to which discussion participants may well have an affinity.

### 3. Specialist accusation - acknowledgement - process argument

(Contextual article, economics section, military affairs specialist)

>I'd also include the French EC725 in your long list – 28 places and a very respectable 5670 kg load, exactly the type they use for floods and fires. The price is 24.5 million USD according to wiki.

>>You're right, Martin, that the EC725 would also match the criteria, and it outclasses the Black Hawk on many parameters. We left it out on purpose because besides France no other European country has it... so it didn't look like a realistic alternative for Slovakia in comparison with the NH-90 or the Agusta.

In this technical discussion about military helicopters, the journalist – typically for a specialist – begins with an acknowledgement, but then defends the framing of the article by restating its purpose – to assess the qualities of the different models the Slovak military was likely to buy. He explained that his inclination to respond is greater when there is a stronger subjective element to information selection and framing – when the authorial input is greater:

> Interview: 'The reader had a good point, but I felt... I had to defend my subjective decision. It was definitely an "author's article", it was our selection and our idea how to process the information. The greater the subjective input, the greater my motivation to follow the discussion and respond. Just because it takes longer than re-writing agency news wires – I worked on that for two days.
> *Researcher: Do you look forward to the public response?*
> I was curious and nervous because a lot of people know what they're talking about when it comes to the army, so they might look on me as an amateur. I want to know whether they'll accept what I've written'.

### 4. Specialist accusation – acknowledgement + authority + process argument

(Contextual article, economics section, railways specialist)[14]

>Mr. [surname of journalist]. Why do you write stupidities. currents can't be in volts. only in amperes. Voltage is in volts! soon we'll be weighing things in litres, won't we?

≫hello, thanks for your observation...we'll alter it in the article.. you're right, of course, that in the case of units we refer to voltage.. when we write up a relatively specialist theme, about which we want to produce a text for the widest possible audience, then in certain places we have to simplify.. sometimes even at the cost of factographics...we can only hope that our readers excuse such simplifications:)[15]

> Interview: 'As I'd deliberately used a different term from the technically correct one, and then some expert among the readers had objected, I'm happy to explain why I chose that term, in the sense of: "you're right, but bear in mind that we don't only write for experts"'.

This is an example of a performative metajournalistic comment (it results in an alteration to the article) which provokes a partial concession from the journalist that he has made an error in a piece about the technical standards on Slovak electrified railways. Nevertheless, following his opening acknowledgment he tries to save face by the juxtaposition of authority and process arguments, the effect of which is to shift the debate onto territory where he is the expert. The shift is signified by the succession of first person plurals, which actually point to different collectives: whereas the phrase 'we refer to' points to the specialist community to which the journalist thus makes an implicit claim of co-affiliation (and confers 'expert' status on the discussant), the phrases 'we write up', 'we want to produce' and 'we have to simplify' point to the journalistic community as he explains how journalism works. The switch from an argument of authority to a process argument is also symbolised by the succession of specialist terms employed: exchanging *voltage* for *factographics* shifts the debate from physics to journalism, and thus onto 'home turf'. The latter three 'we's' might well come over as rather pedagogic, but, as Abbott explains (giving the example of the language used in sponsored legal or medical advice columns in newspapers) a pedagogical tone is common in many of the media through which professional communities strive to maintain public legitimacy.

5. *Internal accusation – External accusation – combined process and authority argument – internal accusation*

(Feature interview in weekend supplement by N's star interviewer)

The following exchange began with a rare intervention by an interviewee (a psychiatrist who has a blog on the N website and is a regular discussion participant) expressing reservations about the choice of headline for the interview:

>Hello. Just to the title of the interview I'd like to add that it's an editorial choice. Straitjackets are no longer used here (I mean above all where I work, but also generally in Slovakia, even though I admit there are regional variations).

>Thanks for your reaction, Doctor. With those straitjackets you've clearly shown (very diplomatically, which only increases your esteem in my eyes) how this 'independent' newspaper manipulates in order to attract readers.

≫ginger, there was no manipulation intended. As Michal himself recalls, and I cite it in the text, he recently came across a straitjacket being used... Let me point out some of the passages that led us to choose this headline [cites from interview]. I don't do this to criticise Michal, whom I hold in great esteem as a specialist and as our blogger, but I have to reject the accusation of manipulation. We've removed the word straitjacket from the headline, even though I insist it was not in contradiction with the text.

The journalist's eventual concession to go with the interviewee's wishes and change the title, however, prompted a new line of attack from the discussant, now bringing a field-internal accusation:

>Changing the name of an article – that's a bad approach. If the reader wants to go back to it (or the discussion to it) in a few days' time, HE WON'T FIND IT, and that's bad – it's a disservice to the reader... And newspapers are FOR THE READER.

At this point the interviewee rejoined the discussion to defend the journalist against both accusations.

>I like the fact that they changed it. It's evidence of flexibility and communication with readers.

Interview: 'I said to myself that nothing drastic would happen – if Michal sees the headline that way, if he thinks the word straitjacket could really mislead readers, then let's change it. And then you saw what happened – that same troll comes back with "How dare you change the headline!" [laughter] Typical situation, when you want to do the right thing so that your respondent is satisfied, and then a reader lambasts you. You can't win either way. And afterwards, of course, people, including some of my friends, asked me on Facebook or by email why I'd changed it, when it clearly follows from the interview that straitjackets can still be used in Slovakia. Lots of people criticised me for that, telling me they'd experienced the use of straitjackets themselves'.

The exchange is interesting for several reasons: the way an intervention by a contributor with a very particular status (the interviewee) can empower other participants' metajournalistic critiques; the liberal use of citations from the article itself to rebut an accusation (a strategy that may relate to a common suspicion among journalists that many people join the discussion without having first read the article, or an allowance for the inability of some readers to read the whole article if – as in this case – it is behind a paywall); the journalist's doubling of authority arguments when he refers to the respondent as both a specialist and a blogger (the latter an identity that could be expected to play well with a participatory audience); and the discussant's switch from an external register (using 'proof' of malpractice to make a generalisation about the manipulativeness of the media) to an internal one – effectively a de-escalation of the critique. Significantly, this followed the success (in performative terms) of the initial accusation, and there is more deference to the institution of journalism in the second intervention by the reader, although this brought little solace to the journalist. That the second exchange was possible testifies to how norms of online journalism are still fluid: changing a headline after an article is published, which was impossible in the pre-Internet age, is not covered by a clear rule, and the same action can thus be interpreted both as a breach of trust with the reader or as reader-friendly. In that sense it can be seen as part of a useful learning process for journalism. The journalist, though, emerged feeling that an attempt to be communicative had weakened rather than strengthened his authority with a part of the public whose opinion he most values, and that it had, perhaps, been unprofessional to exploit one of the Internet's affordances to allow the respondent, via the discussion, to influence a part of news production (headline writing) over which journalism traditionally claims to have exclusive competence. In sharing competence he risked looking incompetent.

6. *Internal accusation – process argument – internal accusation – polemic*

(Double-page exclusive interview with an unnamed whistleblower working in the security services, external correspondent)

>throughout the article one thing doesn't ring true to me, that a colonel from the secret services willingly gives an interview to a newspaper...

≫dear Peter, I don't think the colonel betrayed any top secrets. On the contrary, I didn't get a great deal of answers to my questions.

This initial exchange consists of an internal accusation followed by a process argument, by which the journalist seeks to establish the authenticity of the interview situation, and the fact that the respondent behaved as one would expect a member of the secret service to act.

> Interview: 'what was behind that comment was a moral judgement on my part, that my respondent had behaved correctly'.

There then followed a second exchange, however, in which the contributor continued in the same vein, expounding a critique of the credibility of the source (and by extension the interview) but which drew a different kind of response from the journalist:

>I'm more than ever convinced that this was an attempted infiltration of NATO structures by people connected to the FSB [Russian secret services]; if he praises the Slovak side in the interview and it's obvious that there's a Russian influence in Slovakia, then it doesn't look good.

≫As for what you write about the FSB there's no need to respond at all, I'd recommend watching fewer films and reading some poetry before bedtime instead.

The reader's third contribution took up the polemical lead:

>about the FSB you might try reading the latest articles from Ms. Applebaum [an American journalist who contributes to N] if you can't see what's going on in Slovakia.

The journalist did not reply.

> Interview: 'That's just how I am, I'm really a direct, confrontational person. That has its pros and cons but people coming into the discussion have to realise that I'll go a long way, that I'm not politically correct, and if someone says something laughable I'll make fun of them – I'll let them know about it'.

Discrediting one's opponent is an intrinsic element to polemical discussion, which is not directed towards consensus but towards the rehearsal of antithetical positions that can, nevertheless, inhabit the same space on the basis of a negotiated 'agreement to disagree'. Such an exchange forces each party to take responsibility for their opinions, precisely because the other party refuses to accord them any legitimacy. This responsibility-taking is what the journalist, here generalising about his discussion identity, says he is trying to achieve by *provoking* polemics:

> Interview: 'I'm the one who usually starts the polemic. Most people just pronounce their truth, and a pronouncement's not a polemic. They just state their worldview. I'm the reactive element here'.

He arguably produced a positive effect by provoking a stronger justification – an authority argument citing a source from the same newspaper – in the discussant's third intervention. We are dealing, however, with an unusual case – no other *N* journalist described their discussion identity in quite these terms (the other two polemicists saw themselves in one case as practising argumentation, and in the other as countering what they saw as disinformation and false interpretations). Nevertheless it provides a glimpse of one way in which the conflictual, abrasive, and personal character of online discussion which journalists often lament can instead be embraced in journalism. Precedents for the press giving considerable space to polemical discourse in which social actors, writing under pseudonyms (Feyel 2008: 148), engage in fierce normative conflicts, exist in the *journalism of opinion* of the nineteenth century (De Bonville and Moreau 2004: 332–333) and I argued in Chapter 3 that this paradigm also captures important facets of the journalism practised by Slovakia's 'opinion-forming' press. This type of journalism shares a number of characteristics with contemporary online media systems: a blurring of the 'classical' journalistic commitment to objectivity (nineteenth century papers often even devoted special rubrics to rumours and anecdotes), an imbrication of press and public in collaborative knowledge production, a mixture of endogenous and exogenous discursive genres, primacy of argumentative competences over classificatory and descriptive competences (characteristic of a twentieth century *journalism of information*), and above all pronounced intertextuality in the context of polemical debate both between different media and between the social actors to whom they 'generously open their pages' (Charron and de Bonville 2004: 198). But we could also speak about a return to a dialogical citizen metajournalism, since it was common to find columns in nineteenth century newspapers in which social actors would exchange opinions about previously published news stories (ibid.: 199), a form of intertextuality which, if it did not completely disappear from twentieth-century newspapers, was confined to readers' editor and ombudsman columns, but which has reappeared in online discussion (and social media).

This takes us back to this chapter's central theme: the strange prominence and performativity of metajournalistic commenting practices. Even though they do not often 'degenerate' into polemical exchanges due to journalistic self-restraint, they have an accusatory dynamic that always invites this possibility, and, as we can now see, there is also an historical precedent for this association. Herein lies the heuristic value of studying polemical metajournalistic exchanges: they point to a different way in which professionals can maintain legitimacy, one that Abbott's account of professional discourse omits. Legitimisation (understood here as a struggle for speech rights)[16] occurs here through the adoption of a distinct discussion persona – through engagement in a milieu that is foreign to a journalistic discursive identity and in which conflict, dichotomy and denunciation are legitimate. Other journalists in my sample recognised these situations and typically expressed unease and uncertainty about them:

> I noticed his question, which suggested a certain polemic. I don't know whether I should write something in the discussion in those situations, but here I see I did. (Reporter, culture section)

Most, however, did not, and even here the journalist's response was an authority argument (citing two US sources that countered the discussant's argument) not a direct take-up of the polemical invitation. What, if anything do the three polemicists have little in common? Little in terms of age and experience – one is a deputy editor-in-chief whose articles are mostly commentaries, the second a young and inexperienced reporter on the foreign desk (who had worked as a science reporter until he started at N), and the third an external correspondent, based abroad, whose articles are mostly long-read reportage or occasionally (as in the last example) interviews. A factor they do have in common, however, is a peripherality to their respective organisational sub-fields, one by virtue of having responsibility for the newspaper's online journalism (when the editor-in-chief and other deputies are self-confessed 'print people'), the second by virtue of his recent transfer from a specialist to a more mainstream newspaper rubric, and the third as an external correspondent who combines journalism with another livelihood. This may provide them with a certain incentive or licence to transgress the orthodox.[17] It may orient them towards strategies in which they adopt discursive identities that displace or mask parts of the social identity institutionally accorded to journalists and which define them as competent producers of a certain type of knowledge. They seem to sense that in some situations the way to capture an audience is to hint (at a metadiscursive level) *I'm not what I/they say I am* (Charaudeau 2006). Thus in the following quotation the commentator admits that identity work plays an important part in his discussion contributions:

> I think the first motivation was that the topic struck me as complex and I had some doubts whether I had it well thought out and well-written. That comment wasn't an absurdity or an outburst, it was a legitimate opinion, but it was in conflict with what I'd written, so it seemed worth explaining. Perhaps even for myself: to reinforce my own opinion, or to raise my self-confidence – to show that person I'm on my game. It sounds a little comical but ego plays a big role in writing and it's a bit like that in the comments. (Deputy editor-in-chief for online journalism/commentator)

Tellingly, it is ambiguous here whether it is his identity as a discussant or as a journalist that he is working on when he rehearses arguments to show that he is on his game. I suggest that these situations are so commonplace in a fluid professional domain like journalism that we ought not to see practices in which journalists subvert their scripted roles as unprofessional or deprofessionalising, but as emergent discursive competences; ways in which professionals learn to talk credibly in poorly scripted situations. Such interplay of discursive and social identities is important for professional renewal and innovation, processes through which professions can regain legitimacy at moments in history when they are under public attack, as journalism has been during recent decades. Of course the validity of polemical discussion exchanges may be peculiar to Slovakia and other countries in which the press is strongly implicated in political struggles. But if, as Amossy (2014) argues, pluralist democracies are increasingly organised around difference and conflict (such that consensus is often impossible but coexistence vital), then polemic is a speech mode that has valuable argumentative functions beyond media systems historically anchored in 'political parallelism' (Hallin and Mancini 2004) and these rare glimpses of a third legitimising strategy may have a wider significance.

## Setting Off Metajournalistic Tongues

Not that everyone need read the newspapers but even those who fail to 'are forced to follow the groove of their borrowed thoughts. One pen suffices to set off a million tongues'. (Tarde 1898/1969: 304) (Schudson 1997: 305)

One way of interpreting the rule applied by discussion administrators (see Chapter 4) that comments ought to be 'on-topic', and that off-topicality is a good enough reason for comment deletion, is that journalists share an implicit assumption that the press should set the agenda for public conversations in a very direct, straightforward way. But this chapter's findings about participating journalists' liking for metajournalistic comments imply that if we take a much more selective measure of success or relevance – whether or not the author of an article replies to a comment – then topicality is no longer such a good predictor of comment consecration. Talk about how and why the media covers a topic, evaluations of how well or badly it does so, as well as more general interrogations of the role of the media in society, are what provoke journalists – generally reluctant to respond to readers' comments – to participate. How can we account for this paradox? In a matter-of-fact sense, metajournalistic comments are digressions from the thematically defined topic of the discussion. But I suggest it would not be a distortion of Tarde's image of the press 'setting off tongues' to claim that the media set the agenda for 'vertical' comment exchanges in the sense that they become the agenda, for Tarde understood the relationship between news, public discourse and collective action interactively, making the role of the media dependent on the take-up and treatment of its messages but also its speech forms in conversations.[18]

But there remains a second paradox. In answer to a survey question about what they want from discussing authors, the most active discussants at *N* said that they wanted journalists above all to 'defend their interpretation against public criticism'[19] (72%). In choosing this option they clearly positioned themselves as a critical public when facing the author. They also indicated, however, that metajournalistic debate does not really interest them: only 14% wanted the journalist to 'explain how an article was written'. Participating authors meet this demand half-way: far from ducking criticism, they are indeed more likely to respond to accusations than to praise or neutral remarks. On the other hand, journalists at *N* tend not to respond to (or by) interpretative comments (see Fig. 5.2). Instead they displace the debate to a metajournalistic level (which actually represents a higher proportion of user comments than discussants' survey responses would suggest, but is still a minority commenting genre) and respond to critics of their own work, their organisation's reputation or the integrity of journalism as a profession, using the discussion space above all as an accountability instrument. It's plausible that they do so because, like Swedish editors, asked to assess the importance of different types of media accountability arrangements (Von Krogh and Nord 2010), they do not feel threatened by critical dialogue with their readers when it is about journalism standards (as opposed to critical dialogue about the issues in the news). There's clearly an important space for such discussions in journalism's and newspapers' attempts to work out what kinds of discursive identity retain, or perhaps regain relevance in media systems populated by a more diverse plurality of voices, arguments and communicational competences than ever before. Yet in consecrating a type of comment for which there is relatively modest public demand, they must be careful not to cross the fine line between holding conversations that contribute to media literacy and ones that are just navel-gazing.

## NOTES

1. I discovered the existence of this email because it was remarked on by journalists in interviews, with no apparent resentment towards me for having provided the 'incriminating' statistics, and often with a vagueness that suggested it had only been skim-read.
2. Recall that in this section all articles are supposed to be open for comments.
3. Web-editors do quite often override an author's decision – both to turn discussion on and off – but these are usually unilateral decisions, which can, of course, result in discussion being on without an author knowing. In these cases, the web-editors take charge of administration, but do not contribute. One reporter with a particularly controversial news brief had thought that all his articles had discussion switched off, and only discovered in our interview that several had, in fact, had discussion enabled.
4. Together we looked at the times of his discussion interventions, and, on finding one in the afternoon, he remarked that it must have been a weekend.
5. Recall that 50% of N's internet traffic comes through Facebook.
6. **Information**: provides or requests specific information relevant to the subject of the article.
   **Interpretation**: offers an interpretation of the subject of the article or takes an argumentative position.
   **Witnessing**: describes a personal experience (not necessarily one's own) relevant to but distinct from the event described in the article, qualifies another comment as personal experience, recalls a precedent from a source

of collective memory or expresses opinion as an affected party.

**Metadiscussion**: comments on the discussion itself or evaluates other discussants' competence, attempts to keep order in the discussion, phatic comments.

**Metajournalism**: comments on the process by which the article was produced, evaluates the author's competence as a journalist, or comments on the media in general.

7. In fact that proportion is about 0.5% for all articles by in-house reporters.

8. An interesting exception is the metadiscussion category: although both authors and readers comment equally frequently on the discussion, journalist metadiscussion comments are rarely responses to reader metadiscussion comments. A large number of the latter are phatic comments, whereas the former are more about keeping order.

9. A few comments were actually double-coded.

10. **Internal critique**: accusations of a lack of professionalism: any critique that refers to an ideal model of journalism, against which the actually practised journalism which is the object of criticism is found wanting. Usually employing terminology from the field and criticising the quality of the article based on 'standard' criteria like newsworthiness, objectivity and accuracy, they display a certain deference towards journalism as an institution.

    **External critique**: attacks on journalism as an institution: any critique that contests journalism's jurisdiction over knowledge production, by reference to communicational norms that are 'socially available'. Using vocabulary for writing activities that are not specific to journalism, these comments show an absence of deference towards journalism as an institution and often a cynicism about the interests that journalism serves.

    **Specialist critique**: accusations of a lack of knowledge of the specialist area a journalist covers: any critique in which the comment author declares or displays some expertise in the subject of the article, on which basis they offer criticism that can range from constructive advice to direct attacks on journalism's jurisdiction from the position of a rival profession.

11. **Process arguments**: arguments whose justificatory value resides in a description of the journalistic process, explaining how a topic was investigated, how an article was framed, or sometimes more broadly, how the (Slovak) 'media system' is understood to work. Typically they attempt to demonstrate that actual practice conforms to an ideal.

    **Authority arguments**: arguments that direct readers to a third-party source of evidence, often accompanied by a link. They can complement process arguments (insofar as using and citing reliable sources is intrinsic to journalistic work) but typically, they testify to a felt need to draw upon sources of authority outside the journalistic field that may be more credible in a given context.

**Polemic**: responses that take an antagonistic position to the comment(er), defending the article or the journalist's interpretation against an accusation and typically introduced by a metadiscursive phrase (e.g. 'you're wrong', 'I don't accept that') that prefaces a counter-accusation/argument.

**Acknowledgement**: complete or partial acknowledgement of the merit of the accusation. Typically brief thankyou notes, they concede that the commenter's point is valid.

12. One common reason why specialist articles attract metajournalistic criticism is that a lot of the articles published in economics, culture and science sections of newspapers are reviews or profiles, and are easily attacked as positive or negative PR. Here a process argument is perhaps the only possible defence: explaining the limits of a genre, detailing how the article was put together, or insisting on the provisional character of journalistic knowledge ('if it turns out we were wrong, we'll write about that') were the stock responses to accusations of one-sided product reviews in my corpus.

13. Each example is presented using the following conventions:
    > Discussant's comment
    ≫ Journalist's comment
    Interview: Journalist's interpretation of the exchange during interview.
    Orthographic features such as capitalisation or its absence are retained wherever possible in my translations.

14. In fact it is the same individual as in example 3.

15. The double dots in this comment are authentic, the triple dots indicate a passage omitted.

16. As we could see in the second example, external accusations in online discussion often deny journalists special speech rights – addressing the journalist as the author of a 'contribution' brings them down to the level of any other discussion participant.

17. In Bourdieusian theory an actor who occupies a marginal field position is more likely to turn to external audiences for legitimacy, deploy exogenous resources of cultural capital and claim heteronomous consecration.

18. Tarde would, after all, have been familiar with newspaper rubrics in which non-journalists were given space to comment on the press more than was normal in the century that followed.

19. The survey was sent by email to the 200 most active discussants in a random week in late 2015. 75 questionnaires were returned. The response options to this question were intended to operationalise the same categories by which I coded journalist responses.

## REFERENCES

Abbott, A. (1988). *The system of professions. An essay on the division of expert labor.* Chicago & London: University of Chicago Press.

Amossy, R. (2014). *Apologie de la polémique.* Paris: PUF.

Brin, C., Charron, J., & De Bonville, J. (Eds.). (2004). *Nature et transformation du journalisme. Théorie et recherches empiriques.* Laval (Québec): Les presses de l'université Laval.

Charaudeau, P. (2006). Identité sociale et identité discursive, le fondement de la compétence communicationnelle. *Niterói, 21,* 339–354.

Charron, J., & De Bonville, J. (2004). Typologie historique des pratiques journalistiques. In C. Brin, J. Charron, & J. De Bonville (Eds.), *Nature et transformation du journalisme. Théorie et recherches empiriques* (pp. 141–218). Laval (Québec): Les presses de l'université Laval.

De Bonville, J., & Moreau, L. (2004). Journalistes et magistrats: le concept d'identité discursive appliqué à la couverture de l'actualité judicaire en 1950 et en 2000. In C. Brin, J. Charron, & J. De Bonville (Eds.), *Nature et transformation du journalisme. Théorie et recherches empiriques* (pp. 317–368). Laval (Québec): Les presses de l'université Laval.

Feyel, G. (2008). Une société sans école: histoire de l'invention d'une profession. *Médiamorphoses, 24,* 145–152.

Groenhart, H. (2012). Users' perceptions of media accountability. *Central European Journal of Communication, 2,* 190–203.

Hallin, D., & Mancini, P. (2004). *Comparing Media Systems. Three Models of Media and Politics.* Cambridge: Cambridge University Press.

Schudson, M. (1997). Why conversation is not the soul of democracy. *Critical Studies in Mass Communication, 14*(4), 297–309.

Tarde, G. (1898/1969). *On communication and social influence.* Chicago: University of Chicago Press.

Von Krogh, T., & Nord, L. (2010). Between public responsibility and public relations: A case study of editors' attitudes towards media accountability in Sweden. *Communication, Culture & Critique, 3,* 190–206.

# CHAPTER 6

# Defending the Authenticity of Online Public Spheres

**Abstract** Does the social web permit the spread of rumours and propaganda or the creation of collective critical spaces where they are rapidly tested and disarmed? By looking at what happens when moderation fails and online discussion is 'colonised' by professional political communicators, Smith demonstrates how the publicness of comments spaces renders them both vulnerable and self-regulating. Drawing on pragmatism and ANT, the chapter recounts a successful collective investigation to weed out political trolls with fake profiles along two parallel lines, mapping the semantic history of an item of discussion slang alongside the evolution of routines for controlling online discussion from zonation to traceability. It suggests some preconditions for activating the social web's affordances as a facilitator and not a simulator of critical testing and proving.

**Keywords** Collective investigation · Fake · Propaganda · Public sphere · Social web · Troll

Over the last decade or so there has been a significant shift in public perceptions of how the web deals with propaganda, rumours and disinformation, from a broadly optimistic to a more pessimistic bent, and which mirrors (and doubtless partly explains) the displacement of the positive by the negative myth of participatory journalism. For if, in 2006, Chateauraynaud could write that the Internet 'permits the deployment of collective critical spaces assuring that hypotheses and solutions are put to the test by means of systematic variation – which explains why the duration of hoaxes, rumours and false information is shorter than in the ordinary social world' (2006: 111), today his words may seem a little naive. Even if few would contest the fact that the web offers the *possibility* to create collective critical testing spaces, we increasingly hear (both in media commentaries and in academic debates) several varieties of a counter-thesis. The stark version goes that the web – and in particular the social web – actually aids propaganda, amplifies disinformation and sustains rumours. A more subtle version has it that hoaxes and conspiracy theories thrive on the web not due to the *absence* but due to the *semblance* of collective critical testing. Digital technology and social media are, according to this thesis, good at simulating an experience of testing knowledge and at generating metadata or para- and peri-textual objects which resemble proofs: quantified indicators of approval feign statistical reliability, the surrounding text and images or the visual appearance of a web-page lend credence to the information presented there. Put another way, the 'quality assurance' marks and procedures that attach to knowledge in online networked environments are not as fool-proof as they appear, and can hinder rather than aid discernment. This chapter, limited though it is to an account of a single episode, goes part way to rehabilitating the optimistic thesis, as it describes an example of a collective investigation in which a web-based arrangement for distributed knowledge production more or less did what it was supposed to: it counteracted the scarcity that, in today's information economy, attaches not to 'the body of information created by users, [but] to the technical procedures and social organisations which facilitate its optimal use' (Proulx and Heaton 2011). By attempting, in my account, to describe the full chain of elements that came together to make this happen, I hope to elucidate what some of the preconditions might be for activating the social web's affordances as a facilitator and not a simulator of critical tests and proofs, and specifically for detecting and countering disinformation and dissimulation in online discussion.

## Naming and Accusing False Discussants

From 2008, regular discussion participants on the website of the newspaper *SME* began, with increasing frequency, to voice accusations that some fellow discussants were paid publicists for political parties, covertly seeding the discussion threads beneath certain news articles with propaganda, ruining the atmosphere and disrupting the free flow of debate. Although they sometimes refer to such figures as trolls, they also coined a special pejorative term for such a contributor (brigádnik), which eventually became established in the local discourse of *SME*'s comments threads and blogs as an expression of disquiet, a term of denunciation or a signal to others of the illegitimacy of certain participants. The term was used, metadiscursively, to regulate the debate. During the same period what I shall call the system of vigilance that oversees the discussion at *SME* underwent a gradual re-equipment – shifting, as explained in Chapter 4, from a system based on quality control to one based on reputation control or, applying a metaphor from public health, from a zonal system to a traceability system. What I want to show in this chapter is how these two processes converged: how the innovation of a set of routines for controlling online discussion to the news intersected with the semantic history of an item of discussion jargon. Episodes like this, I suggest, can tell us much about the vulnerabilities and resilience of socio-technical systems when faced with threats to the integrity of discourse in the public sphere.

In order to produce a description capable of interweaving a cognitive/semantic and a social/organisational account I draw upon two methodological traditions: pragmatism and actor network theory. From the former I borrow the notion of investigation or inquiry, in the sense intended by one of the founders of philosophical pragmatism, Charles Peirce. Investigations are routinely launched in problematic situations, either when the 'quality of life' and '*vivre ensemble*' of a milieu or community is disrupted or when a problem assumes a level of complexity that demands the mobilisation of a transversal 'community of inquiry' oriented towards and limited in duration by the collective need to solve the problem. Solving the problem means making sense of the situation and working out how to work together (Lorino 2007) – producing knowledge and producing a group. In sociotechnical environments, however, we need to think of the group and the process of working together in the spirit of actor-network theory – the active association of heterogeneous elements through a process of *intéressement* and enrolment (Callon 1986). I show how a system of vigilance – defined as a sociotechnical arrangement emerging and reconfiguring around the definition and attempted solution of problematic situations, made up of actors (occupying the roles of operators and sensors), physical and symbolic objects, routines and arguments (Chateauraynaud and Torny 2013; Cefai 2009) – complexified over time through such a process.

The sociology of controversies has shown how most investigations start from intuition and other tacit forms of knowledge (Chateauraynaud 1996: 65), but one of the most difficult problems of collective inquiry is the relationship between intuition and proof. Intuition – the word is derived etymologically from vision – denotes perceptions or convictions obtained from watching something attentively (from practical sense) without (yet) being able to furnish any tangible proofs. Chateauraynaud defines it as a register of experience-based knowledge that has still to find an adequate interpretive framework or 'calculation space' – the space in which you test knowledge and which defines the criteria of proving (2004: 17). Expertise, in fact, is often manifest (made public) by the retrospective equipment of intuition with a formal justification (Leroi-Gourhan 1964: 89). There is, however, an equally important feedback mechanism at work: proof regularly remodels intuition, changing our way of seeing (Wittgenstein 1983: 150). Intuition and proof therefore have to be connected in a recursive loop to ensure system reactivity, which happens, according to Peirce, through cycles of inferential reasoning in which three fundamental types – abduction, deduction and induction – are successively mobilised. That is what happened, in the following case, when the organisational trajectory of an actor-network converged with the semantic trajectory of evolving practices of naming and accusing. Successive enrolments of actants, resources and routines enabled the system of vigilance and its operators to make better use of their own and the sensors' intuition in the generation of acceptable proofs.

The pejorative term referred to a moment ago, when fully spelled out, is the phrase 'brigádnik zo Súmračnej', which means 'temp from Súmračná street'. Súmračná street is the address of the headquarters of the political party Smer-Social Democracy (Smer-SD), which, under the leadership of Prime Minister Robert Fico, has headed the Slovak government for all but two years (2010–2012) since 2006. The phrase insinuates that someone in the discussion is working for this party and is thus not a genuine discussant. Between 2008 and 2013 this phrase occurred 154 times in online discussion in the newspaper *SME* and 57 times in the texts of complaints or alerts sent to the discussion administrators and its use increased markedly from the second half of 2012 (see Fig. 6.1). It is not a phrase that has ever appeared in the newspaper itself, and that is the first reason why I was interested in it – as an example of discussion slang, a term coined and adopted by discussants themselves to describe an endogenous discussion practice, specific to Slovakia, and largely (but not exclusively) to *SME*. It also points us for a second time towards accusations, now not against the media and journalists for their normative transgressions and other alleged shortcomings but against discussion participants for infringements of discussion standards and ethics. A third source of interest is that the invention and growing usage of the term contributed towards the visibility of a phenomenon – covert seeding of online discussion by political parties with the apparent intention of influencing public opinion by artificially generating positive PR – and to its installation as a public issue. It is an issue which has parallels in other parts of the world (notably the so-called troll factories allegedly organised by regimes like Russia and China) and in other spheres (e.g. the mass generation of fake, product-friendly comments by commercial companies). Some regard such practices as a significant threat to democracy and to the authenticity of the public sphere.

The solid line on Fig. 6.1 shows the distribution of occurrences of the phrase 'brigádnik from Sumračná' over time, based on a search of *SME*'s online archive of articles, blogs and discussions conducted in January 2014.

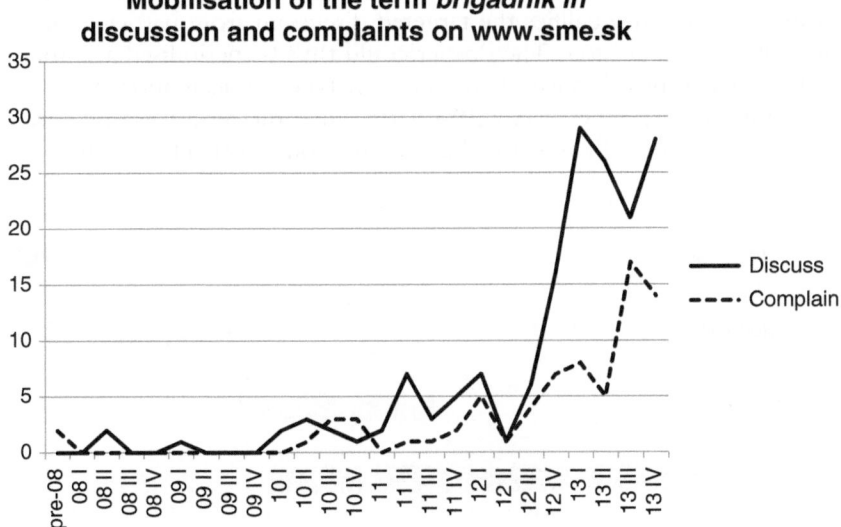

**Fig. 6.1** Occurrence of the phrase 'brigádnik zo Súmračnej' on www.sme.sk by quarter

The term was used for the first time in the second quarter of 2008, reoccurring only sporadically until 2011, before becoming much more widespread during late 2012 and early 2013. What the graph therefore shows is that the term's adoption as part of the common lexicon of participants in the online discussion space at *SME* was a process that began slowly and then accelerated, before seeming to plateau out towards the end of the observation period, in the manner of a typical diffusion curve. I also searched the database of alerts sent to administrators to report inappropriate comments, and the dotted line on Fig. 6.1 shows that use of the term 'brigádnik' in alerts increased at a similar rate to the discussion (without accelerating to quite the same degree in 2012). The numbers are small[1] but they are a useful indicator of comment performativity, since we know what decision the administrator took in each case. In effect we can infer the perlocutionary force (Austin 1962) of the term from the level of agreement between alerter and administrator.

I coded the search results from the discussion archive to differentiate the types of accusation being made. Unlike in the metajournalistic accusations (see Chapter 5), the initial typology was derived inductively by observing the recurrence of a number of tropes in discussants' formulations. Each register could be captured in a simple phrase or proposition expressing what disqualifies the targeted discussant from participation in the eyes of their accuser. The dossier could thus be periodised according to the relative prominence of the different types of accusation, which is shown in Fig. 6.2 (the years 2008–2010, when the term was only rarely used, are omitted). In an early phase, accusations most often related to a

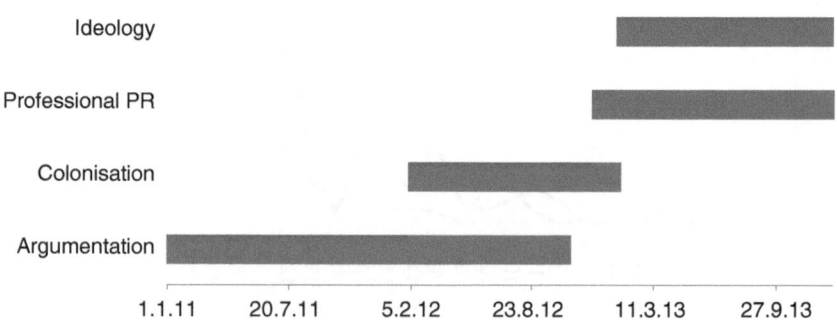

**Fig. 6.2** Timeline of accusatory registers

discussant's style of argumentation, implying that arguments are either flawed or predictable and formulaic, as in this example:

> [s]hould you not be arguing how your idol has improved the situation of the airport? Throwing around a few certified facts and figures about increases in number of flights? Have you run out of arguments, brigádnik? (27.4.10)

But during a second phase, essentially covering 2012, accusations more often reflected an intuition that the public sphere was being 'colonised' by political marketing:

> I love how brigádniks immediately congregate around the blogs of politicians like Paška [then speaker of Parliament for Smer-SD] pushing everyone else aside with a flood of reactions, one to another. Always the same template. (27.2.12)

Then, beginning in late 2012 and lasting throughout 2013, there was a third phase when the most frequent type of accusation targeted the professionalisation[2] of communication. These accusations included a lot of ironic remarks about the overall activity of brigádniks, as participants in the discussion began to 'normalise' the phenomenon. For example, around the turn of the year 2013 we find these two comments in the discussion:

> I see it's a party holiday for the brigádniks from Súmračná. (27.12.12)
> The brigádniks from Súmračná are really trying hard today – maybe they've been promised a bonus and that's why they're joining in so actively. (3.1.13)

An ideologically tinted accusatory register also showed a rapid rate of increase in 2013, coinciding with a shift in the course of the investigation, when the finger of blame was pointed squarely at Smer-SD as the party responsible for 'polluting' the discussion. The following example illustrates how holding certain opinions was sufficient to draw an accusation:

> Welcome back, red brigádnik from Súmračná, we missed you. Desperation and frustration ooze from your calls to tax, regulate and restrict, just so that the government has as much as possible to redistribute to its sponsors through over-priced tenders, artificial government jobs and similar forms of stealing. (18.5.13)

Two minor accusatory registers are not shown on the diagram: the term brigádnik was occasionally also mobilised to support accusations focusing directly on other discussants' identity (e.g. '*another brigádnik from Súmračná with a computer-generated name*' (30.6.13)) or else featured in counter-accusations defending the plurality of the public sphere (e.g. '*Rhetorical questions. Today I'm quite happy to be labelled a brigádnik from Súmračná to have a go at your hypothetical reflections.*' (12.9.13))

What is particularly notable is how the four dominant accusatory registers correspond to different forms of reasoning, as shown in Table 6.1, and one can say that the change over time in the tone of typical accusations – the semantic trajectory – has a logical progression in keeping with the metaphor of a police investigation or detective story. A suspicion emerges (from a combination of observations and inferences or intuitive leaps), then there are attempts to generalise about its importance and implications using inductive reasoning (categorising and generalising about the consequential effects for the public sphere). Finally, there follows a period when deductive reasoning gains the ascendancy and observed cases are reinterpreted from the perspective of general rules (the connectors 'therefore' and 'because' often indicate the presence of deductive steps in the third and fourth registers). A second general trend concerns the 'unit

**Table 6.1** Forms of reasoning in the accusatory registers

| Period | Accusatory register* | Form of reasoning | Unit of analysis |
|---|---|---|---|
| 2008–2012 | It's not qualified to be here because the **argumentation** is flawed! | Abductive | Message (comment) |
| Early 2012–early 2013 | It's a **colonisation** of the public sphere by political marketing! | Inductive | Message (discourse) |
| Late 2012–end of 2013 | You're **professional PR** people, and therefore morally disqualified from participation! | Deductive | Messenger |
| 2013 | You're not entitled to be here because your **ideology** does not fit this community! | Deductive | Messenger |
| *Minor register* | *You're not entitled to be here because you're using a **false identity**!* | *Deductive* | *Messenger* |
| *Minor register* | ***Disagree** here and you get labelled a brigádnik!* | *Inductive* | *Message (discourse)* |

*These phrases attempt, at the risk of over-reduction, to typify the sense of each accusation.

of analysis': we witness a shift from accusations that target arguments (the speech act) to those that target individuals (the speaker). The 'professional' register, notably, is invoked to delegitimise protagonists, and the investigation culminates when the 'ideological' register (as well as the minor 'identity' one) is invoked to 'profile the suspect' or typify the perpetrator. The counter-accusations seem to resist this trend, representing fleeting and ultimately vain attempts to restore a focus on the message rather than the messenger, and using inductive reasoning.

To make full sense of this sequence we need to combine discourse analysis with an analysis of investigative routines. There were three central routines relevant to the investigative process: two were active throughout the observation period, but the third only took shape during the second half of the investigation.

## User Intuition as a Reputation Management Routine

The first routine it is important to consider covers the day-to-day reading and interaction practices of regular discussion participants. It was by reading the comments and interacting with other users on a regular basis that some users began to suspect that not all others were 'genuine':

> There's a narrow group of 'hard-users' who are there daily and know the community, know who's been around for years and are perhaps sensitive to those kinds of things – if new names start cropping up regularly, if they only appear under certain topics or if they use the same arguments over and over. (Interview with project manager for user-generated content at *SME*, February 2014)

They reacted both by reporting suspicions to administrators and making public accusations in the discussion, and we can regard these metadiscursive discussion contributions as a spontaneous externalisation of intuitive knowledge. One notable characteristic of this knowledge is that it attaches to people (or more accurately, to user IDs) more than to messages. The very term brigádnik (on a grammatical level) names a person rather than a thing, but more particularly the comments and alerts that use it often indicate that their intelligence comes not just from reading a single comment or a series of comments in a thread, but from clicking on a user profile and perusing the reverse chronological list of all the comments made by that user. Despite this, however (cutting back to the semantic account), the initially predominant accusatory register denies or corrects this attachment to the person: discussants usually framed their accusations around the content of messages, focusing on types of enunciation attributed to brigádniks and on how, because their speech allegedly failed certain tests in terms of its level of argumentation, it 'polluted' the space of the discussion threads and merited deletion. It is as if it were still taboo to attack the person.[3] We might attribute this to the type of inferential reasoning being mobilised: to a reflexive awareness among discussants that they are working abductively; to a peripheral uncertainty about these early intuitions; to a sense that the investigation was at an early stage in the testing of evidence.

## Admining as a Quality Control Routine

Chapter 4 described the work of web-editors in the *SME* newsroom who adjudicate alerts received by discussion users. They were therefore the people who first became aware when users began to use the term brigádnik as a justification for alerts. There were two contrasting types of alert: sometimes, particularly in the early period, people objected to the use of the term 'brigádnik', viewing it as an abusive expression, especially when directed against them. They were often classified as a 'personal attack', and their justifications either simply quoted the offending text or followed the template: 'I am (X is) a decent discussant, and Y is calling me (them) a brigádnik!' A more general version of the same complaint objected to the use of the term per se, classifying comments that used it as 'spam' (implying the term itself was an indicator of political marketing, part of the PR wars between supporters of political parties). But the more frequent type of alert, which was almost completely dominant in the final two years, demanded the deletion of a comment (or even the blocking of an account) on the grounds that its author was suspected to be a 'brigádnik'. These accusatory alerts were often classified as 'other breach of the codex', indicating that the threat perceived to the order of the discussion was distinct from those that the rules anticipated. Figure 6.3 thus indicates how usage of the term changed over time. Initially what predominates are *objections* to its use from discussants who regarded it as an unwarranted term of abuse. Later, objections become relatively less frequent, replaced by *accusations* in which the term is employed as a label for an unacceptable practice. From being itself a breach of etiquette, brigádnik became a shorthand way of calling attention to a breach of etiquette.

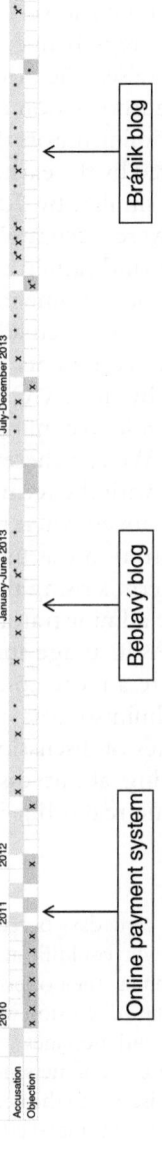

**Fig. 6.3**  Timeline of alerts using the term brigádnik[4]

*Note:* X= comment deleted by admin; *= account blocked by UGC project manager

The two types of alert had different success rates. Whereas administrators normally acceded to an objection,[5] the frequency with which an accusation was upheld is overall much lower. Significantly, however, it shows an increase over time. The step-change occurred around the turn of the year 2013. Something had raised the power of the word to carry a forceful accusation and the (self) authorisation of administrators to act on it; something had convinced the administrators that the new term captured an unacceptable practice not covered by the existing discussion codex and/ or that an increasing proportion (similar, by 2013, to the overall success rate of alerts) of such accusations were 'accurate'. This is shown in Fig. 6.3 by the increasing number of Xs (indicating a blocked comment, or a successful alert) in the upper row of the timeline. Indeed Fig. 6.3 shows that the 'accuracy' of the accusations was actually greater than the success rate of alerts: the asterisks indicate comments by users whose discussion accounts were eventually blocked by the UGC project manager (a procedure described later) when he was able to confirm that they belonged to an organised network of discussants. We can therefore see that during 2013 the majority of comments labelled with the term brigádnik in an alert were either blocked or subsequently removed when the system was cleansed at the level of user accounts. User intuition was usually 'accurate'.

Part of an explanation for the term's rising performativity (its ability to trigger a comment deletion by the administrators) undoubtedly lies in the semantic history of a new word. As its usage spread in the discussion, we can assume that it began to acquire a more consistent meaning, one that came to be understood by the administrators and regarded as a credible way of categorising 'other' breaches of discussion rules. It became part of the accepted vocabulary for talking about discussion. But part of the explanation lies not in the semantic realm but in the newsroom routines for regulating discussion:

> I had no reason to intervene in the early days because I couldn't be sure they weren't just complaints from people who couldn't stand up for themselves in the discussion and therefore tried to eliminate their opponent by getting the administrator involved … At that time online discussion was a problematic project for *SME* since there were 10 to 12 thousand messages a day. So even if there were a dozen people [brigádniks] writing dozens of messages a day on certain themes, it was not a problem for us in comparison with the need to find and remove truly vulgar messages, messages that seriously infringed ethical standards or broke the law. (Interview with UGC project manager, February 2014)

In this quotation, the UGC project manager describes why complaints about brigádniks were treated as trivial until early 2013. Aside from issues of task prioritisation, two other things stand out in his assessment: the inadequacy of the investigative routines and detection devices to make decisive judgements about who was and who was not a brigádnik; and the focus on the message as the administrators' unit of analysis. Messages were (or were not) problematic at this stage, not discussants. As we saw in Chapter 4, this relates to the way the very routine of discussion administration unitises the discussion into messages (the object of alerts), which are usually adjudicated without considering the wider context of the discussion thread or inspecting the credentials of the discussant in more detail, mainly due to lack of time and because the main organisational concern is to ensure that the discussion contains no potentially libellous content rather than to discipline or guide discussants.

Since the attention of administrators is focused on the message they have a low level of awareness of the overall profile of discussants, and did not identify brigádniks in the course of performing their daily routines. This contrasts with the gaze of regular participants ('hard-users'), whose reading practices gave them a better intuitive grasp on an emerging phenomenon. For the main limitation on the informational value of user discussion histories or environmental clues is available time and interest, of which the 'hard-users' have considerably more.

## Verification as a Credential-Checking Routine

Organisational routines for managing the discussion were not constant during the observation period. The most significant change occurred in May 2011 when *SME* joined a scheme to charge for certain types of online content known as Piano. This affected the discussion, since unlimited access to the comment areas of the *SME* website was thenceforth restricted to subscribers, whereas non-subscribers could post a maximum of three comments per day. This lent a new dimension to the verification of user identities. Initially account requests and modifications had been handled automatically via an email confirmation system. This had already been switched to a manual task in an attempt to encourage people to use their real names, with the incentive of being able to link their discussion account to their blog[6] (interview with deputy editor-in-chief). Now there was an additional reason for scrutiny, and the task was assigned to the recently appointed UGC project manager. Each morning he would go through a list of user account creations or amendments waiting for approval. One of the principal checks was to ensure that new accounts are not duplicate accounts for a user already registered under another nickname, since this was an obvious way of avoiding payment for the right to post more than three messages per day. The routine therefore involves cross-checking personal identifiers: names, nicknames, email addresses, cookies and IP addresses. What is being tested is the authenticity and uniqueness of a new user ID. Another variation of the verification routine is performed retrospectively, that is, not on new accounts but on existing ones. It starts by tracking cookies to detect 'groupings' of discussion accounts with very similar names or created one after another:

> there are three forms of payment evasion: the creation of multiple accounts in a short time (with the intention of using them in the same discussion), accounts with the same nick, just a different number at the end (so that other readers can tell it's still 'him'), or accounts created shortly after someone had written their third contribution of the day – here, too, there's a clear intention to evade payment (email communication from UGC project manager no. 2,[7] May 2016).

Normally these routines have no direct connection to the administration of discussion, but after it was discovered that it had inadvertently caught some of the brigádniks, the UGC project manager reasoned that Piano provided a useful source of intelligence, and that he could easily adjust his morning verification routine for explicitly investigative purposes.

The trigger for that displacement was a blog post.[8] On 25th February 2013 an opposition MP Miroslav Beblavý published a blog[9] purporting to describe how discussants working for Smer-SD operated. It concentrates (like the first accusatory register) on reconstructing the argumentative strategy of a brigádnik, citing eight imaginary rules deduced from a month's worth of discussion which Beblavý had had his parliamentary assistants code and analyse. They include, for example, intervening below articles that personally implicate Smer politicians in order to defend their reputation, hinting that one has privileged information or insight about the political scene, and repeating the term 'stability' in relation to government policy. He said he was trying to reconstruct what an instruction manual for hired discussion participants might look like. Beblavý's eight rules 'made sense' to the administrators at *SME* and furnished them with a new resource – a set of tests that could be applied to help identify a brigádnik. They helped to frame admins' judgements, themselves partly intuitive (as seen in Chapter 4) and align them with the intuition of discussants, if we regard Beblavý as a sort of super-user. His evidence was likely to be particularly credible to *SME* for several reasons: his conclusions were based on 'hard' research, he and his party were ideologically closer to the newspaper's editorial position than Smer-SD, he had the status of a 'VIP blogger' on the *SME* blog portal and before entering politics he worked at the economics think-tank INEKO, a frequently cited source in *SME*.

His guidelines confirmed the practical sense of discussion administrators, but they were not particularly useful in isolation since they dealt in discourse and semantics, and their unit of analysis was the message. In order to link semantic to social networks it was necessary to enrol data from the online payment system. In effect this data was used in following up discursive evidence – suspicions raised at the comment level either by an alert from a reader or by administrators' own checks[10] – in order to reveal wider networks. This investigative work became part of the UGC project manager's verification routine:

> once we'd identified a person as unwanted, as part of that network, we blocked all the other (discussion) accounts connected to the same Piano. I reasoned that we weren't blocking accounts, we were blocking people – people we'd decided we didn't want in the discussion. (Interview with UGC project manager, February 2014)

The introduction of the online payment system provided the technical means to intensify surveillance over users, and helped realign the system of vigilance from quality control to reputation management. By the spring of 2013 *SME* was confident of detecting and blocking such accounts within 24 hours of their creation. The cells in Fig. 6.3 marked by an asterisk refer to comments from accounts eventually blocked by this investigative procedure. Altogether more than 200 were blocked during the rest of the same year.

Pausing here to consider each of the three routines – hard-user intuition, discussion administration and account verification – we can see that while they overlap, the broad sequence in which they were mobilised also traces an investigative cycle, this time following a sequence modelled on science – where induction serves to test, experimentally, predictions deduced from a hypothesis based on abduction. (Chauviré 2010: 48). The intuition of hard-users equates to abductive reasoning (producing conjectures about the conditions that could have produced an observed fact), the administration routine (at least in its ideal form) to deductive reasoning (checking conformity of facts with rules) and the verification routine with inductive reasoning (making associations and spotting patterns among a plurality of evidence). It is also striking how the sequence of routines mirrors the trajectory of accusations by passing from an impersonal to a personal register. In contrast to the original two routines, credential checks and their associated resources (the UGC project manager, the online payments system) deal in user identities rather than their speech acts. So we see a gradual reconfiguration of the system of vigilance in order to detect and punish people (discussants) instead of just judging and where necessary deleting comments, while at the same time the accusations of discussants go through a parallel shift of target. Perhaps there is a mutual reframing of the problem: the new *dispositifs* give discussants new ways of grasping the phenomenon and change the way they can formulate their accusations, while conversely the changes in the way they express their intuitions enable and legitimise the reconfiguration of the 'calculation space' according to a corresponding logic and with the effect, I argue later, of according a more important place to users' experiential knowledge.

## A New Calculation Space

A second 'VIP blogger' intervened in the controversy a few months after Beblavý. Radovan Bránik is a less well-known public figure, closer to the stereotype of the activist blogger. His posts often seek to make an issue overlooked by the media into a public issue, for he feels that the Slovak media is often too conservative in its judgements of newsworthiness, cowed in the face of political or economic pressures (interview with Bránik, 2014). There is often a polemical flavour to his posts. The one he published on 2 November 2013[11] drew 227 comments and 1,265 Facebook recommendations. With over 40,000 page views it had four times the average readership for his other blog posts and ranks just outside the top 200 most-read blog posts of all time on the *SME* platform. In it he exposed three fake pro-Smer-SD bloggers. He had performed a simple investigation to confirm his suspicions, contacting the schools, universities and employers mentioned in the bloggers' profiles or their linked Facebook pages and discovering that none of these organisations recognised their names. He also made contact with the *SME* blog administrator, who told him that the three blogs all came from the same IP address. His central accusation – in a text that cleverly parodied an urgent appeal for a missing person – was that if organised participation in online discussion is reprehensible, but perhaps unavoidable in an anonymous environment, the creation by political parties of false identities on blogging platforms and Facebook is a much more serious threat to the public sphere, and what is more should be preventable if proper checks are performed by the host servers when people register. It was the shift between platforms – from comments to blogs – that, in Bránik's judgement, incurred a more serious infraction of online communication ethics.

But most important for present purposes was what ensued over the following days in the discussion beneath his blog post. Aside from many expressions of support and thanks, he got volunteers in an improvised programme of civic surveillance. Other discussants turned into helpers in a spontaneous and distributed collective investigation. For example, they used photo recognition software to search for stolen identities and analysed patterns of links between profiles on social networks, managing to uncover several other fake identities and pointing towards some of the possible organisers among politicians. These revelations produced an instant reaction from the accused parties, who 'went to ground' and tried to hide their tracks by deleting their blogs and Facebook profiles. In real time, a game of hide and seek ensued: as blogs and Facebook profiles were disappearing, the citizen investigators took screenshots, downloaded photos and copied text to preserve the evidence, the 'chase' accompanied by a running commentary in the discussion thread. They did not, however, spare the host medium from criticism. For example, one discussant commented: 'it's a disgrace for the admins at *SME*, isn't it? That when someone registers they don't even carry out a basic check that their photo isn't stolen. What's the point of the rule that you have to blog under your own name and photo if no one verifies it even on a trivial level?' (tt.) Another wrote: 'what disappoints me most is that the admins do nothing about it, but they throw you out of the blog for any old excuse. What's the ethical codex for?' (jakobin).

Administrators at *SME* then found themselves in a difficult position. Called to account on two different measures of professional competence – the adequacy of diagnostic procedures and the speed of implementation of treatment measures (Abbott 1988) – they faced an external jurisdictional challenge: they needed firstly to demonstrate greater efficacy, and secondly to respond to an implied claim that the abductive inferences of hard-users were at least as good as the formal inference procedures on which professions base their jurisdictional claims. The UGC project manager voiced this dilemma as follows:

> It's true that we can't meet the high expectations users place on administrators ... even if people think we have more power than we really have. That's just something we've got to come to terms with. On the one hand I'm grateful for what happened in the discussion under Bránik's blog, where people criticised us for the fact that some bloggers had evaded our checks. I acknowledge it was our mistake, but I would add, on the other hand, that people don't know how many other cases we've found and dealt with in the course of our routine controls. (Interview with UGC project manager, February 2014)

The professionals' disadvantage, in effect, was the invisibility of 'successfully resolved cases' in comparison with the cases publicly named and shamed in the discussion. Blogger and discussants had, in effect, opened a new calculation space capable of turning conjectures into proofs, which both rivalled and complemented the official calculation space of discussion and blog administration. The reaction was a partial, but temporary collaboration: their proofs were accepted and acted upon, with a fresh wave of blocked blog and discussion accounts. But a tension remained between different ways of knowing and standards of proof, symbolised by the term that was appended to the blocked accounts in the internal information system: 'strike force Smer'. Admins could have adopted the indigenous discussion term, brigádnik. But choosing their own 'stopgap label' (Abbott 1988: 51) served to reaffirm jurisdiction over the investigative process, by distinguishing the 'professional' diagnosis from users' inferences, and to terminate a logical chain of inferences when action was urgent.

## PROTECTING ONLINE PUBLIC SPHERES: ZONAL MONITORING AND MOBILE VIGILANCE

The main motif of the episode described in this chapter is a double convergence: between the semantic and organisational trajectories of investigation, and between the agendas of discussion administrators and hard-users. For the latter's demand for a democratisation of vigilance to make it more open to intuitive expressions of disquiet converged with the administrators' work re-equipping the system of vigilance with more powerful routines and resources, focused more on reputation management than on quality control. The strengthening of the verification routine and the de facto adoption of Beblavý's eight rules enabled and authorised discussion administration to give more weight to intuition-based warnings, reputational status indicators and embodied common sense wisdom in the organisation of participation rights in online discussion. The original configuration of the system of vigilance governing online discussion was founded on isolating the speech act. The new configuration recognised that a discussion community operates according to a different perceptual schema focused on the qualities ascribed to other users/members of the milieu: the trust and distrust they express towards one another. And, crucially, it was capable of enacting credible procedures to track and assess reputations.

The difference is akin to that between competing models of public health security, one based on enforcing zonation and if necessary quarantine (Foucault 1977) and one based on securing the traceability of networks and movements. The argument is often made that the second has displaced the first in many types of public health threat, since it is better adapted to the level of mobility of people, products, parasites and diseases in a globalised space-economy (Torny 1998). It is instructive to draw an analogy with the routines discussed in the present case in order to explain how the routine of administration, founded on a principle that it is possible to use the alerts submitted by users as a basis on which to 'zone' the discussion into more and less dangerous areas and then to isolate and expel dangerous messages or threads, was outflanked by the mobility of users between *SME*'s discussion forums and other interconnected regions of the Slovak social media ecology. Procedures that took advantage of the intrinsic traceability of digital identities[12] – the verification routine exploiting metadata gathered for commercial reasons, the blog discussants' collective inquiry exploiting web-based identity tools and linking user accounts across social media platforms – proved more adept at detecting and eliminating the danger. The admin routine was already shifting from quality control towards reputation control, as described in Chapter 4; but only when user intelligence was factored in could the system of vigilance for online discussion fully exploit the affordances of digital networks to counter disinformation.

But if there are cases, like this one, when it is easier or more effective to maintain control by tracing a mobile network than monitoring a fixed space, the administration routine may be more effective at dealing with other threats to the order of the discussion, the principal ones remaining incivility that discourages participation and the newspaper's potential legal liability for content that breaks the law. One of the key differences is the speed of reaction required: even if the UGC project manager boasted that brigádnik accounts were generally eliminated within 24 hours by late 2013, that would be far too long a reaction time for dealing with complaints about offensive content, since the 'damage' to the quality of a discussion thread propagates within minutes as discussants react to one another. After 24 hours, most threads are already dormant. The alerts routine is able to react much more quickly precisely because it works on a principle of zonation and isolation that enrols users in a different capacity – as witnesses of what is happening right now in a defined space.

Effective systems of vigilance rely on somebody being 'simply present' (Chateauraynaud 1996: 82). They also rely on devices for tracing mobility that has risen to an unprecedented level in digital networks. The routines and resources of the 'system operators' – the administrators – make them present in a different kind of space than the one in which discussants act. Precisely because they have a zonal, context-poor, bird's-eye perspective, they rely all the more on crowdsourcing in the sense of continued attention and action (Haythornthwaite 2009) – on the experiential knowledge and mobile vigilance that users obtain by participating in online discussion and learning to follow its traces across a network. A precondition for this is strong commitment to and investment in the collective enterprise, without which it would scarcely be possible to interest users as sensors, emitters of alerts and collective investigators – in the co-production of both quality control and reputation management. In this type of virtual 'crowd/community',[13] participation extends beyond merely taking part and expresses the idea of contributing to something and benefiting from being part of something (Proulx 2015). For Zask, taking part is the recurrent, normal, sociable phase of participation 'when the advantages of association rather than its inconveniences are predominant' (2011: 322); contributing and benefiting (giving and taking a part) come more into play in exceptional or foundational phases, when the existence of a group is less taken for granted or less available and has to be interactively (re-)modelled, (re-)negotiated or (re-)contractualised. They are metadiscursive phases in the life of a collective entity. If that is in fact what was going on in this episode, then we have met another manifestation of metadiscursivity, in a very functional form: a function of a communitarian form of life online, and of its crises, expressed as an ethic of care for the technical apparatus that makes interaction possible and gratifying (but which is no less strongly attached to artefacts and routines for that). What is more, metadiscursive activity was performative – it was recognised and rewarded by the professional curators of the online environment, altering the way they came to think about quality control:

> When I saw the reactions of all the discussants under [Bránik's] blog, it was very reassuring in the sense that it proved that this community had somehow managed to keep itself going, to regulate itself without relying on the administrator … [It shows that] even if we make a mistake there are loads of other readers who are not just readers but contributors, active participants of the discussion who can moderate our mistakes … I admit they were very adept, that community … There is a self-purifying process [through which] together with this community we can improve the quality of the environment … We couldn't manage it without a community to whom it matters. (Interview with UGC project manager, February 2014)

Of all the examples of participatory journalism examined in this book, the brigádnik controversy provides us with the closest fit we have seen between professional (expert) and amateur (user) knowledge practices. Nevertheless, even as it partially reconfigured the system of vigilance, recalibrating its calculation space to enable new forms of critical testing and proving adequate to the threat posed to the authenticity of the public sphere by an orchestrated campaign of disinformation, it did not produce a stable, institutionalised accommodation. The collaboration of discussants and administrators 'under' Bránik's blog was a one-off mobilisation: it did not remain open as a 'calculation space' even if it is reasonable to suppose it could be revived. The *SME* discussion rules have not been recodified to add 'brigádnik-ing' (identity dissimulation or organised discussion) as a category of offence, nor has there been any change to the formal division of roles between participants, in the direction of the kind of user-moderator models employed, for example, by Slashdot or Civil Comments. A more apposite image is a temporary alignment between groups of actors with distinct programmes of action around a specific common problem (Cooren 2004). That is not to diminish its importance. In fact at least two aspects of this episode – intersecting programmes of action and metadiscursivity as a focus on governance problems in a joint action space – are emblematic of the way that different epistemic cultures (Knorr Cetina 1999) learn to work together in a range of transversal knowledge production regimes (Smith 2015).

## Notes

1. Recall that alerters are not obliged to add a written justification and usually only tick one of the four standard categories – vulgarism, personal attack, racism/xenophobia or advertising/spam.
2. In the sense of turning an activity into paid employment.
3. Personal attacks are one of the four categories of practices banned by the *SME* codex.
4. The timeline also places three key events, whose significance will be explained in the following sections.
5. In most cases they came from the target, and administrators might therefore give some weight to subjective perceptions of harm.
6. The blog section has a strict real name policy.
7. The job changed hands in January 2015.
8. For a more detailed account of the brigádnik controversy as a series of 'alerts' and 'affairs' in the media and the blogosphere see Smith (2014).
9. http://blog.etrend.sk/miroslav-beblavy/osem-pravidiel-brigadnika-smeru-2.html [accessed 7.7.16].
10. Following Beblavý's first rule they started to scrutinise the discussion below articles about leading personalities in Smer-SD.
11. http://branik.blog.sme.sk/c/341131/Zachrante-blogera-Mareka-Albrechta.html [accessed 8.7.16].
12. Digital identities often come equipped with the kind of 'external memory' (Torny 1998: 57), or metadata, that public health specialists have to arduously construct, for example by getting victims to fill out questionnaires about their movements and contacts.
13. Such a crowd may not be a community, but it is 'assembled in the interests of community' (Proulx and Heaton 2011).

## References

Abbott, A. (1988). *The system of professions. An essay on the division of expert labor.* Chicago & London: University of Chicago Press.

Austin, J. (1962). *How to do things with words.* Cambridge, MA: Harvard University Press and London: Clarendon Press.

Callon, M. (1986). Some lements of a sociology of translation: Domestication of the scallops and the fishermen of St Brieuc Bay. In J. Law (Ed.), *Power, action and belief: A new sociology of knowledge?* (pp. 196–223). London: Routledge.

Cefai, D. (2009). Comment se mobilise-t-on? L'apport d'une approche pragmatiste à la sociologie de l'action collective. *Sociologie et sociétés, 41*(2), 245–269.

Chateauraynaud, F. (1996). Point de vue de Francis Chateauraynaud. In L. Boltanski, F. Chateauraynaud, & J.-L. Derouet (Eds.), *Alertes, affaires et catastrophes. Logique de l'accusation et pragmatiques de la vigilance? Actes de la cinquième séance du Séminaire du programme* Risques Collectives et Situations de Crise (CNRS). Grenoble: Maison des sciences de l'homme, 54–85.

Chateauraynaud, F. (2004). L'épreuve du tangible. Expériences de l' enquête et surgissements de la preuve. In B. Karsenti & L. Quéré (Eds.), *La croyance et l'enquête. Aux sources du pragmatisme* (pp. 167–194). Paris: EHESS (Raisons pratiques, n° 15).

Chateauraynaud, F. (2006). Moteurs de (la) recherche et pragmatique de l'enquête. Les sciences sociales face au web connexionniste. *Matériaux pour l'histoire de notre temps, 82,* 109–118.

Chateauraynaud, F., & Torny, D. (2013). *Les sombre précurseurs. Une sociologie pragmatique de l'alerte et du risque.* Paris: EHESS.

Chauviré, C. (2010). Aux sources de la théorie de l'enquête: la logique de l'abduction en Peirce. *Revista Colombiana de Filosofía de la Ciencia, 10*(20–21), 27–56.

Cooren, F. (2004). The communicative achievement of collective minding: Analysis of board meeting excerpts. *Management Communication Quarterly, 17,* 517–551.

Foucault, M. (1977). *Discipline and punish: The birth of the prison.* New York: Vintage Books.

Haythornthwaite, C. (2009). Online knowledge crowds and communities. Paper Presented at *International Conference on Knowledge Communities,* Reno: University of Nevada. Available at: https://www.ideals.illinois.edu/handle/2142/14198 [accessed 10.7.16].

Knorr Cetina, K. (1999). *Epistemic cultures: How the sciences make knowledge.* Cambridge, MA: Harvard University Press.

Leroi-Gourhan, A. (1964). *Le Geste et la parole. Technique et langage.* Paris: Albin Michel.

Lorino, P. (2007). Communautés d'enquête et création de connaissances dans l'organisation: le modèle de processus en gestion. *Annales des Télécommunications, 62*(7–8), 753–771.

Proulx, S. (2015). Usages participatifs des technologies et désir d'émancipation: une articulation fragile et paradoxale. *Communiquer, 13,* 67–77.

Proulx, S., & Heaton, L. (2011). Forms of user contribution in online communities: Mechanisms of mutual recognition between contributors. In J. Pierson, E. Mante-Meijer, & E. Loos (Eds.), *New media technologies and user empowerment* (pp. 67–81). Brussels: Peter Lang.

Smith, S. (2014). Alerts and affairs in the 'brigádnik' dossier. The trajectory of public problems in (and beyond) online discussion spaces. *Human Affairs: Postdisciplinary Humanities and Social Sciences Quarterly, 24*(4), 423–436.

Smith, S. (2015). Multiple temporalities of knowing in academic research. *Social Science Information, 54*(2), 149–176.

Torny, D. (1998). La traçabilité comme technique de gouvernement des hommes et des choses. *Politix, 11*(44), 51–75.

Wittgenstein, L. (1983 [1939]). *Remarques sur les fondements des mathématiques.* Paris: Gallimard.

Zask, J. (2011). *Participer; essai sur les forms démocratique de la participation.* Paris: Le bord de l'eau.

# CHAPTER 7

# Conclusion

**Abstract** Returning to the book's unifying conceptual themes – routines, arguments and competences – Smith uses extracts from a member-checking interview with a key informant to stage a dialogue between his research findings and the practical concerns facing journalism at its present participatory turn. He argues that the notion of convergence culture does not capture what is needed for participatory journalism, understood as a collective accomplishment. Everyone is not a journalist but everyone can be a contributor to an orchestrated polyphonic performance, as long as the distinctiveness of their knowledge resources and competences is respected in socio-technical arrangements that allow for both routinisation and improvisation.

**Keywords** Argumentation · Competence · Contributor · Convergence culture · Routine

In a pragmatic coda to my research – in order to both test my conceptual tools and explore some of their 'conceivable practical effects' (Peirce 1934) – I undertook a member checking interview with a key informant from the field, the former UGC project manager at *SME* who later moved to *Denník N* as their social media editor. Here I use extended extracts from our interview[1] to structure a final consideration of my three key themes. In a play with words, I refer to him as my discussant and, pursuing

© The Author(s) 2017
S. Smith, *Discussing the News*, Palgrave Studies in Science,
Knowledge and Policy, DOI 10.1007/978-3-319-52965-3_7

the parallel with the socio-technical system of commenting (even if we are now, perhaps, closer to the academic type of discussant), I invite readers to make the same choice that faces a time-pressed discussion administrator and either leave him in virtual anonymity so as to focus on the message, or follow a trail of hyperlinks (starting from the endnote) that progressively uncover a digital identity. The link also serves as a way of acknowledging his de facto co-authorship of this concluding chapter and invaluable contribution to the book as a whole. Each sub-section of the conclusion begins with a recapitulation of key findings or arguments from the empirical chapters.

## THE ESSENTIAL 'LIVENESS' OF ROUTINES

At the risk of oversimplification, my conception of routines outlined in Chapter 3 can be reduced to the following heuristic: we can learn something about the evolution of professions by studying 'routinisation', but we learn more, both about professional and organisational dynamics, by studying routine performance and scripting as generative systems. To illustrate this point, let me first return to the 2015 redesign of *SME*'s admin interface and the situations when admins persisted in looking for the reputational indicators that had disappeared from the main interface for admin work. Rather than seeing this as resistance to change we can, with recourse to a generative understanding of routines, view it as creative adaptation to a discrepancy between the artefact available to them and their grasp of the routine 'ostensively': since judging reputations as well as message content still belonged to their internalised guide for routine performance, they worked around the new artefactual constraints. Even if two of the new admins, who only rarely 'clicked through' to user histories, acted more in accordance with the new design features (allowing their performance to be nudged more strongly by the way the artefact had been redesigned), the capacity of performance to diverge from the 'dead' routine inscribed in an artefact reaffirms how little control designers have over routines, especially if an organisation invests very little in the ostensive (Pentland and Feldman 2008: 247), with no training, no opportunities for collective rehearsal or consultation and no behavioural incentives. But there are good reasons for this in *SME*, where variability is not perceived as a problem so long as it concerns only diverging patterns of action without producing bad decision-making. 'All's fine as long as we're not being sued', was how some managers would half-jokingly explain their attitude to discussion administration. The laissez-faire attitude of managers can even be interpreted as a willingness to treat the web-editor admins as professionals and accord them corresponding discretion as to how they perform the routine. In this context an artefact (the interface) is not a strong constraint on action. Indeed its affordances as an enabler of routine performance rather than a 'routiniser' are what strikes the observer. The routines I observed in the newsroom involved improvisation and variety: it was during the very performance of routines that actors found and exploited the 'discretionary space' that one commonly associates with professionalism. Inference did not start when routines stopped, inference happened within routine performances.

Complaints about routinisation occurred in a different situation: when a substitution of one artefact for another prevented the reproduction of a work routine that was valued and internalised for the space it afforded for creativity – for its 'liveness'. When *SME*'s former UGC project manager sought to re-enact the admin routine after moving from *SME* to *Denník N*, he found himself unable to do so, and the barriers were technological rather than organisational. Prompted to compare the two interfaces, his vocabulary follows the ordinary understanding of routines that Abbott employs, but the processes he describes reflect Pentland & Feldman's idea of routines as generative systems:

> When we migrated from the system we had at *SME* to that very basic Wordpress system, which didn't support anything at all except for the option of deleting a comment – the user didn't even need to register and thus have an account and a history – I really appreciated how important technology is in enabling you to try things. At *SME* we could try moderated discussion, we could work out what specific transgressions warrant blocking an account, and so on. But when you've got useless tools then any change, anything outside the routine is constrained by that fact, and the whole of an admin's work gets reduced to deleting the worst examples, and what's more it takes 95 percent of his time – in fact it takes twice the time that it does with a supportive system. And all the plans we had for the discussion in the first few months at N were thus postponed, in fact cancelled, because we couldn't do anything with a system like that: all our work went into chasing a few dozen people who were able to cause us so much trouble that it occupied all our administrative attention and capacity. That's why I see technology as crucial and that's when I realised how much it influences my decision-making and

the steps I perform. At *SME* I would look at IP addresses and cookies, we tracked whether users had multiple accounts and other things that I can't do here. Just performing the basics is so different depending on whether a person has an enabling system or not.

What he says he liked about the old artefact at *SME* was the way it enabled improvisation around or within the standard routine (performative variation) as well as enabling him to contemplate design changes to improve or extend work routines (ostensive variation). Conversely, when he describes the two interfaces he has experienced at N as 'routinising' he is actually indicating a negative perception of the artefacts. He sees them as inferior because there are certain tasks he wants to perform – the 'reputation control' aspects of admin work such as checking, banning and warning users or pre-emptively checking their credentials on registration – that he defines as going 'outside the routine', but which it would be possible to describe as the creative aspects of 'live' routines. The lesson is this: a good tool (like that which I observed in the *SME* newsroom) is supportive, allowing you to routinise standard procedures but also facilitating easy 'referral' to inferential judgement in the non-standard cases and even prompting the design of new patterns of action; a bad tool constrains your options even in non-routine situations and thus incapacitates frontline knowledge workers when they need to deal with many of the everyday realities of human complexity. The socio-technical arrangements for participatory journalism should permit a combination of routinisation and improvisation.

## VENUE-SENSITIVE ARGUMENTATIVE REGISTERS

Studying how arguments were deployed and tested in online discussion and its moderation confirmed the common impression that argumentation practices in online discussion often diverge from the rational, dialogical models prised by journalism to include argumentative registers that are more conflictual, more emotive, more personal, more rhetorical, more ad hominem. The result is to destabilise familiar categories (of newsworthiness and public value) and frames (for public problems) rooted in journalism's informational paradigm. But it also showed how argumentation, in these circumstances, is particularly reflexive: it is accompanied by a running meta-argumentative commentary from participants, which can be used as an indicator of what kind of epistemic culture might be emerging in the hybrid spaces of news comments.

Asking my discussant what he valued about online discussion produced a predictably equivocal response, reflecting the doubts about the argumentative competences of the public that are widespread in contemporary newsrooms. But, speaking as an experienced observer of online discussion to news, he also ventured a genuine appreciation of argumentative distinctiveness and diversity.

> Personally I relish discussions that are entertaining. I don't really expect lengthy academic debates that are going to offer me inspiring thoughts or change my perspective on something – that's all fine, and there's probably too little of it, but often it's just simple fun. You get situations that you don't expect at all, when jokes and little conversational nuggets surface. Or when two completely disparate worlds clash and I can follow that conflict – that's where the power [of discussion] lies; those are the moments which prompt me, as a reader/spectator, to share something on social networks or take a printscreen. When someone writes something stupid, firmly convinced he's right, and then gets his come-uppance from others, using humour, wit or arguments to take apart his 'truth' – that's a beautiful discussion moment. And you also get moments that resemble those in the pub, when a group of friends improvises a running commentary on the TV news. Sure, there are well-argued contributions and those that bring new information, but I guess I don't go to the discussion for that. Partly because of what I know about how people read online news: I'm well aware that they often just skim-read articles for the basic information, and I think it's probably the 'fun' aspect that motivates those people to take part in the discussion.

Having initially defined discussion by what it is not, or what it will, in his view, always be at best a poor replica of, he asks us to respect the characteristics of the venue, and in contrast to the preamble to *SME*'s moderated discussion rules the occasional resemblance of new online venues to 'pub debates' is not seen as a disqualifying attribute. While he does indeed invoke the term argumentation to characterise a form of speech that is under-represented, if we adopt a broader, pragmatic definition of argumentation it is possible to interpret his words as implying that 'argumentatively strong moments' (Chateauraynaud 2011: 118) *are* available in online discussions, but they are characterised by conflict, parody, humour and wit as well as by 'arguments' in the narrow sense of (logically or factually) justified propositions. Indeed – given what he knows about website navigation patterns – superficially good arguments are to be treated with the same suspicion that courtroom lawyers might regard them with. But nor is he praising unjustified propositions: in fact he says that what he enjoys most is their deconstruction by opponents who, however, employ techniques other than a justified proposition to counter-argue.

Humour and parody can be ways of engaging with uncomfortable subjects that would be excluded from sociable conversations (Min 2016), and Amossy (2011) has proposed the carnivalesque as a model for online news discussion, 'a space voided of all consecrated truth and liberated from the norms of ordinary politeness, where ideas are incessantly tested and contested irreverentially'. Nevertheless it's important not to lose sight of the news in these digital conversations: Schudson (1997) and Katz et al. (1993), both drawing on Tarde, argued that if conversations are the necessary recontextualising devices that enable the press to influence public opinion, the inverse also applies: 'truly public' conversation, the kind that transcends mere gossip, can scarcely exist without the framing of public problems by the mass media. Even if discussants might only have skim-read the news, they pick up its frames, which are often more overtly encoded in the paratext than in the text of an article. I think it's the same kind of interactive, iterative and parasitic relationship between news and talk about the news that fascinates my discussant: it's their symbiosis that makes possible certain types of argumentation which – in his judgement – make it still worthwhile braving the comments space.

## An Orchestrated Distribution of Competences

Participatory competences were studied indirectly, through the ways in which they are monitored, evaluated, conferred, withheld and otherwise managed by online newspapers, in particular by the administrators of discussion spaces below the news. My analysis found that administrators apply different quality criteria to user-generated content from those used to judge the newsworthiness of professionally produced content: thus they did not expect the same discursive competences from non-journalists as they do from journalists (in their other capacity as web-editors). Secondly, it found that their judgements related as often to the author as to the content of a message – that, it was as much about reputation control as quality control – even when technological arrangements were altered in ways that might have constrained this tendency to embody or attribute discursive competences. But, and this is my third important finding, the reproduction of participatory competences also took place in a rather complex division of labour, which positions admins as arbiters in a quasi-legal system of vigilance, but retains an irreducible place for ordinary participants, mobilising users' attention as the system's sensors. Users, generating alerts, are the only actors who can initiate the process of judgement by denouncing, accusing or complaining. Hence the judgement of discursive competences always begins with a 'peer' judgement, before the official arbiter is summoned.

With such a system, in point of fact, the ideal participant masters both discursive competences and quasi-legal ones. Here the discussion codex plays an important role as a mediator or boundary object enabling cooperation between discussants and administrators. Effectively, if you don't have a system that distributes some of the vigilance work to users, there's little need to have written discussion rules because their basic communicative function disappears. It is in the cooperative resolution of alerts that a discussion codex undergoes the tangibility tests that make it an actant in 'live' routines. Hence the surprising fact that N, despite its commitment to participation, has not bothered to draft any discussion rules has a simple explanation: the discussion system at N has been able to go without a written codex because it lacks an alerting system and does not ask participants to display quasi-legal competences. This relieves the social media editor of the 'dispute resolution' workload that occupied much of his time at *SME*. Rather than welcoming this, however, he felt that there is a lack of accountability in a system without a metadiscursive dialogue of complaining between users and system operators:

> At *SME* I regularly had to exchange emails with someone, complaints came in about blocked accounts, but in a year at N there's been nothing similar. Partly because I can't block accounts. But I don't even get the moral and legal threats about how we've run the discussion that used to come to me at *SME*. Which is another reason why we've had less motivation to create a codex.
>
> *Researcher:* But couldn't it be that complaints came in at *SME* because people had a codex to rest on?
>
> It could well be – and that's how it should be. We need people to complain when we've made a bad decision, and they need some rules if they're to do so.

An engaged fourth estate, so to speak, demands a monitoring fifth estate. Since the logical next step would be to distribute still more of the labour to users – to take advantage of their evaluatory competences – by implementing 'community' models of moderation or administration, I asked my discussant if these had been considered during his time either at *SME* or *N*:

> *Researcher.* Haven't you considered distributed models like Slashdot[2] and Civil Comments,[3] where community members partly take over the admin role?
>     *We're not at that point yet, although perhaps if I'd remained at SME…Here we lack the programming resources for that. You need the support of a programmer, it's not a one-off thing, you have to optimalise and adjust the system. But I'm following Civil Comments closely, I'm in touch with them, I've been asking if they're planning any foreign language mutations and when they'll have it in a more advanced state, because their system's still running in beta-version. And if they don't want too much money it's something we might go for.*

He thus saw the main barriers to community-based discussion administration not in any lack of competence on the part of users but in technological and human resource factors, and in the dependent position of a media organisation in a small national market. This sense that Slovak media are no longer in a position to be innovators and must wait until products have been road-tested in more advanced markets contrasts notably with the situation in the early days of participatory journalism, when *SME* in particular, was willing to take risks. At the present conjuncture commenting is both relatively standardised and yet increasingly criticised due to concerns about discussion 'quality' and its economic and democratic value. There are doubts about the participatory competences of the public, which, allied to the standardisation of artefacts and the stabilisation of a division of labour for handling online discussion, make it difficult to contemplate new rounds of innovation 'in the east' even as dissatisfaction mounts in newsrooms.

Journalistic competences are often portrayed as experience-based: developing a 'nose' for a story, being able to perceive an 'event' where an ordinary observer sees only a sequence of activities, deciding rapidly in the field which leads to pursue, whether a source is credible or what questions to ask are often cited as the type of skills that cannot be learned from text-books. They become reflexes and automatisms, and they are inferred from practice, internalised, and only then externalised in codes, scripts or curricula that often seek themselves to replicate conditions of practice modelled on real-world situations rather than deduced from theory (Charron and De Bonville 2004: 39). Rules, or rather rulemaking, has historically been mimetic in journalism, accomplished through observing the practice of more experienced colleagues during a period of 'initiation' (at the micro-level) (Pelissier and Ruellan 2003) or through observing and imitating rival media (at the meso-level of a media system) (Boczkowski 2010). At the same time, and athough journalism incorporates a wide range of genres, there is, for some, an irreducible intuitiveness about most journalistic writing that distinguishes it from technical forms (Cornu and Ruellan 1993), an irreducible place for creativity, flair and instinct that is essential to many journalists' subjective feeling of competence, and which culminates rather than wanes as a journalist gains experience – as they become a more competent professional (Charron and De Bonville 2004: 53).

This revealed itself in many research situations. For example, when I asked journalists about the rules they followed in relation to online discussion (particularly about when or how they respond to comments) I was sometimes frustrated by their inability or unwillingness to generalise – by their insistence that these things are very 'unpredictable', 'specific' or 'spontaneous'. One of my research techniques, however, made use of journalists' natural tendency to relate competence to situated experience: when I invited interviewees to look at examples from their portfolios, I found they often needed very little further prompting to engage in moments of knowledge externalisation (Nonaka and Takeuchi 1995). Confronted with these examples (see Chapter 5), they inferred rules about what they were trying to do and what competences they needed to do it, often prefacing responses with a phrase like 'I'd never thought about it properly until now'. A commentator spoke of practising, performing, displaying and testing his own argumentative competences in the discussion, and while he was atypical both in his willingness to respond to comments and in his willingness to experiment with unorthodox discursive identities, his remark speaks to a facet of participatory journalism which holds true beyond his own case: its function as a rehearsal space for both 'improvisations' and 'standards' (to borrow a musical metaphor), finding out what works communicationally, demonstrating 'good practice' and intersubjectively testing who can do what, where and how. The groundedness of competences in situated experience comes across very strongly in my discussant's reflections on what journalists can and cannot do – and what they allow themselves to attempt – in the space below the news:

*Researcher.* What kind of internal dialogue do you have when considering whether and how to respond to a sharp criticism?

*I'd never really thought about it. I like to follow the discussions, but I don't often join in, I'm your typical average reader, a consumer of content most of the time. I react if something really amuses or really annoys me. People express a range of opinions under my articles but mostly I don't feel the need to comment, steer, add or expand. I'm not the type who has to have an opinion on everything. But then there are cases that provoke me, whether it's someone casting doubts on my work or moments when I see that the person's completely wrong, or that he's brutally wronged me, and I feel that if I don't speak up the others might think that he's right. So for the sake of my professional integrity, for the sake of my name, for the sake of the work that's behind the article it's sometimes necessary to mention certain things, maybe things that I didn't include in the article, to prevent that opinion arising. To defend my name, my work, my employer, myself, the essence of the article, the essence of the theme.*

Researcher: OK, but how do you decide how to react?

*Maybe I react in those moments when I know how to react – that's it! When I see a comment and in the same second I know what to write, I have a clear opinion and I'm already formulating thoughts and words, or I know what source to link to. If it doesn't call forth a stream of words then I let it go.*

Researcher: Are there ever comments that you think about and come back to later?

*For sure, those are the controversial themes and the criticisms of our work. Then I might consult a colleague or my girlfriend, ask them what they make of the person. It depends on what situation I'm in, what's happening at that moment, if I'm bored or enjoying myself, so I can't give a straightforward answer to your question.*

Researcher: Maybe the point of the question was to what extent is a journalist free to adopt different identities in their articles and in the discussion? Do you think it's more important to be consistent or to adapt your style to the environment?

*That's a question that's preoccupied me for years, since I started blogging. I write differently when the boss commissions a piece for the print edition, differently when it's my own theme – then I'm usually writing for the web – differently again for my blog, in terms of the choice of headlines and the wording. And I think I react differently in the discussion, too. Because in each case I'm in a different role.*

The multiplication of roles that goes with the advent of a convergence culture between channels for news in the digital environment requires the mastery of a corresponding multitude of journalistic competences, and since discussion is just one in a series of spaces in which journalists appear and communicate with the public, there's little difficult or unnatural about the idea of varying one's discursive identity for someone working at the digital hub of a converged newsroom. One simply adds another string to one's bow.

But some observers worry that discursive hybridity may be at the expense of professional authority, if it makes journalistic writing less distinguishable from advertising, marketing or ordinary conversation (Neveu 2009: 104). My discussant agreed that some of his colleagues who have reservations about discussion and social media are acting under an imperative of consistency that is an expression of their professional identity, particularly in the case of reporters, whose identity is rooted in the informational journalistic paradigm:

> The strict divide between commentary and news gets totally disrupted on social media: the moment you share your own article, with the words you use to promote it, you're already becoming engaged and subjective. If some colleagues feel an internal brake there, I think that's a good thing.

New jurisdictional claims (the extension of journalism into peripheral spaces that they share with 'amateurs') can thus be renounced in the name of a professional identity that depends, like any other, on self-discipline. Here the division of labour in the newsroom enters the equation as a crucial factor in the reproduction of a collective competence to perform participatory journalism. Not all good journalists of the participatory era have to be conversational, interactive, friendly and informal (Marchionni 2013), collaborative, connecting and facilitating (Ahva 2012), nor must all journalists necessarily master generic hybridisation and multi-layered intertextuality in their writing. Not all the boundary work going on around digital journalism is 'expansionary' in Gieryn's terms (1983). Perhaps it's fair to say that good journalism relies more than ever on carefully coordinated teamwork – which extends beyond the boundaries of news organisations, while still depending on having 'reliable primary material' or 'certified information', whose production requires a certain protective insulation both from the economic imperative of immediacy (Neveu 2009: 105) and from the din of incessant online conversations.

The peripheral roles and unthankful tasks assumed by journalists when they perform participatory journalism assume their value in mutual concertation. Sometimes they get deployed selectively and sequentially as part of a repertoire of discursive identities that an individual adopts as they move between different milieu and thus – as with the polemicists in Chapter 5 – can help them learn to talk credibly in poorly scripted situations; sometimes, as in Chapter 4, they get deployed as part of a multi-task job description which demands the ability to switch between different evaluation criteria for web-editing work and admin work; but ultimately they always get deployed as part of a division of labour for a certain type of knowledge production whose effectiveness and social authority depend on the coordination of distinct components, including non-journalistic actors and actants (as spectacularly demonstrated in Chapter 6), but must guard against their mutual assimilation. In Chapter 4 I argued that the lack of contact between admins and their clients is a missed opportunity for extraprofessional legitimacy work that would benefit the profession; but conversely there are figures in the newsroom for whom professionalism will continue to mean limiting their contact with the public. They are those closest to the 'abstract' pole of professional work, but given a well-coordinated division of labour, they too have a stake in participatory journalism.

If we look on participatory journalism as a collective accomplishment, perhaps it is words like orchestration or polyphony, which Cardon (1995) invoked to describe what he observed around another participatory *dispositif* – the radio phone-in – rather than the term convergence that best capture the relationship between journalistic and participatory competences. As to the question of competence-as-jurisdiction, the slogan 'everyone a journalist now' might be better replaced by the idea that 'everyone is a contributor now', following Zask's (2011) stipulation that participation is only contributive if each participant retains the possibility of making and claiming a difference through their intervention, and is thus valued for their distinctive knowledge, role or work. Such a neutral term – a boundary object – would accord dignity to professionals and amateurs without obscuring their essential differences or the jurisdictional divisions that make their cooperation possible, and which are possibly all the more important in media systems that are paradigmatically hybrid, mixing elements of the journalisms of information, communication and opinion. The opinion-forming discourse of the news organisations studied in this book is a collective voice, based on divisions of labour within the newsroom, and gaining in authority if an effective division of labour is also configured between journalist-contributors and citizen-contributors in the participatory production and discussion of news.

## NOTES

1. The full interview is available (in Czech) at: https://dennikn.sk/blog/vytvorili-jsme-monstrum-nezajimali-jsme-se-ne/ [accessed 12.12.16]
2. On metamoderation at Slashdot: https://slashdot.org/faq#meta1
3. For an introduction to Civil Comments' crowd-sourced moderation system: https://www.civilcomments.com/

## REFERENCES

Ahva, L. (2012). Public journalism and professional reflexivity. *Journalism*, *14*(6), 790–806.

Amossy, R. (2011). La coexistence dans le dissensus. *Semen*, 31. Available at: http://semen.revues.org/9051 [accessed 16.2.16].

Boczkowski, P. (2010). *News at work: Imitation in an age of information abundance*. Chicago: Chicago University Press.

Cardon, D. (1995). Comment se faire entendre? La prise de parole des auditeurs de RTL. *Politix*, *8*(31), 145–186.

Charron, J., & De Bonville, J. (2004). La notion de paradigme journalistique: aspects théorique et empirique. In C. Brin, J. Charron, & J. De Bonville (Eds.), *Nature et transformation du journalisme. Théorie et recherches empiriques* (pp. 33–56). Laval (Québec): Les presses de l'université Laval.

Chateauraynaud, F. (2011). *Argumenter dans un champ de forces. Essai de balistique sociologique*. Paris: Éditions PÉTRA.

Cornu, D., & Ruellan, D. (1993). Technicité intellectuelle et professionnalisme des journalistes. *Réseaux*, *11*(62), 145–157.

Gieryn, T. (1983). Boundary-work and the demarcation of science from non-science: Strains and interests in professional ideologies of scientists. *American Sociological Review*, *48*, 781–795.

Katz, E., Maigret, E., & Dayan, D. (1993) L'héritage de Gabriel Tarde, Un paradigme pour la recherche sur l'opinion et la communication. *Hermès*, *11–12*, 265–274.

Marchionni, D. (2013). Journalism-as-a-conversation: A concept explication. *Communication Theory*, *23*(2), 131–147.

Min, S.-J. (2016). Conversation through journalism: Searching for organizing principles of public and citizen journalism. *Journalism*, *17*(5), 567–582.

Neveu, É. (2009). *Sociologie du journalisme [Troisième edition]*. Paris: La Découverte.

Nonaka, I., & Takeuchi, H. (1995). *The knowledge-creating company. How Japanese companies create the dynamics of innovation*. Oxford & New York: Oxford University Press.

Peirce, C. (1934). *Collected papers of Charles Sanders Peirce, Volume V: Pragmatism and Pragmaticism.* Cambridge: Harvard University Press.

Pélissier, N., & Ruellan, D. (2003). Les journalistes contre leur formation? *Hermès, 35,* 91–98.

Pentland, B., & Feldman, M. (2008). Designing routines: On the folly of designing artifacts, while hoping for patterns of action. *Information and Organization, 18,* 235–250.

Schudson, M. (1997). Why conversation is not the soul of democracy. *Critical Studies in Mass Communication, 14*(4), 297–309.

Zask, J. (2011). *Participer; essai sur les forms démocratique de la participation.* Paris: Le bord de l'eau.

# INDEX

© The Author(s) 2017
S. Smith, *Discussing the News*, Palgrave Studies in Science, Knowledge and Policy, DOI 10.1007/978-3-319-52965-3